## ADDITIONAL PRAISE FOR *ZAITOUN*

"A big bowlful of delicious Palestinian recipes, plus lots of insightful and moving stories."
—Yotam Ottolenghi

"Yasmin Khan is a human rights campaigner and storyteller as well as a recipe writer, and the three strands of her work are illuminatingly woven into this, her new book, *Zaitoun*, an important collection of recipes and stories from the Palestinian kitchen. This is a politically engaged and hungry travelogue, and it is also an inspirational recipe book, and one that anyone who loves food will want to cook from, will need to cook from."
—Nigella Lawson

"As a Palestinian who grew up in Jerusalem, I have been conditioned to be wary of any non-Palestinian trying to share our story and our culture with the world. . . . Very quickly I found myself in tears at just how beautifully and accurately she has captured the essence of our Palestinian culture. Yasmin Khan you have done Palestinians and our story justice, your understanding of the nuances of our culture and history is unparalleled."
—Reem Kassis, author of *The Palestinian Table*

To all the Palestinians who generously opened up their homes and hearts to me.
Thank you for teaching me about beauty, resilience, hummus and hope.

YASMIN
KHAN

# ZAITOUN

**Recipes *from the*
Palestinian Kitchen**

Recipe photography by Matt Russell
Travel photography by Raya Manaa' and Hosam Salem

W. W. Norton & Company
*Independent Publishers Since 1923*
New York · London

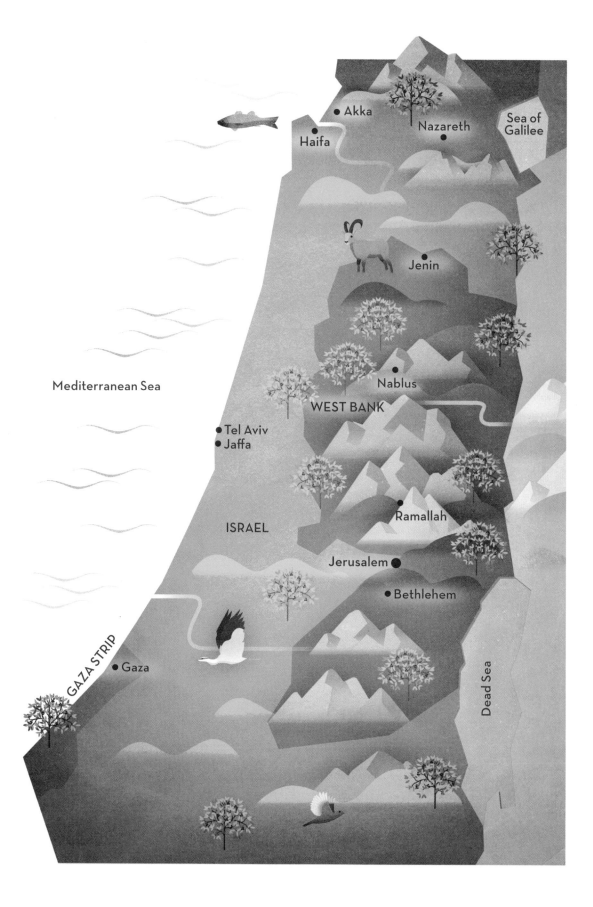

Mediterranean Sea

Akka
Haifa
Nazareth
Sea of Galilee

Jenin

Nablus
WEST BANK

Tel Aviv
Jaffa

ISRAEL

Ramallah

Jerusalem
Bethlehem

Dead Sea

GAZA STRIP
Gaza

# Palestine and me

I'm an adventurous eater and curious traveler, never more at home than when in an unfamiliar food market, captivated by the bustling sounds and scents of a foreign land.

Fortunately, my two careers have enabled me to do both. When I was a human rights campaigner, I traveled the globe, collected stories from people I met and translated them into campaigns for justice. As a food and travel writer, I travel the globe, collect stories from people I meet and translate them into recipes for celebration. The thread running through all my work is a fundamental belief that humans, wherever we are in the world, have more to unite us than to divide us. Celebrating this commonality is my passion, inspired by the old Jewish adage that 'an enemy is just a person whose story you haven't heard yet'.

It was this desire to share stories that first took me to Israel and the West Bank in 2009, while working for a British human rights charity.

It wasn't the easiest of trips. Nothing prepares you for seeing the physical apparatus of the Israeli occupation of the West Bank at close hand: the checkpoints, the walls, the soldiers, the refugee camps. I found the days hard to digest and the pain of the traumatized communities difficult to bear.

But the evenings brought respite. As night fell, my troubled mind was distracted by my greedy stomach. Deep bowls of thick hummus arrived at the dining table, rich with tahini, smooth as silk. Smoky eggplant, roasted over charcoal and smothered with garlic and lemon, had me reaching for a third helping. Vibrant herb salads. Crunchy pickles. Olive oil so peppery that it's the only seasoning you need. The flavors sang on my tongue: sharp, salty, fresh and bright. Palestinian food tasted alive. And in a region that too often feels as though it is dying, I appreciated that more than ever.

I came back from that first trip to the Holy Land convinced I'd never tasted such flavorsome produce and, to this day, I have yet to find tomatoes that taste as good as they do in the Fertile Crescent. I've traveled through Israel and the West Bank three times since, each journey teaching me more about the flavors and fragrances of the Palestinian table and the realities of everyday Palestinian life.

———

But what is the Palestinian kitchen? As I write, there is no country called Palestine, it hasn't existed since the British Mandate of Palestine ended in 1948. But the national and cultural identity of the people has never waned and neither have the delights of the cuisine. Today, pockets of the Palestinian kitchen can be found all over the world, from Bethlehem to Beirut, Berlin to Brooklyn.

Around 4.5 million Palestinians live in what the United Nations refers to as the Occupied Palestinian Territories (OPT). This consists of the West Bank, Gaza and East Jerusalem. More than 4 million Palestinian refugees live in Jordan, Syria and Lebanon, making Palestinians the largest refugee population in the world. Around 1.5 million Palestinians remain in Israel and approximately 1.5 million more live elsewhere in the world.

For the purposes of this book, I chose to focus on exploring the cuisine and food culture of the Palestinian communities I visited on my travels within Israel and the OPT. This book is not intended to be an exhaustive travel guide, but rather it reflects places I was personally drawn to for agricultural, culinary and cultural reasons. I was not able to reach Gaza, as it is blockaded by the Israeli authorities, with no movement of goods or people into or out of the Gaza Strip, and so I visited the Gazan kitchen by cooking in people's homes elsewhere in the diaspora.

———

A note on the voices included in this book. During my years of visiting this region, I have worked with Israeli NGOs and grassroots groups, stayed in the homes of Israeli friends in Tel Aviv and enjoyed the culinary skills of talented Israeli chefs at home in London and in New York. I have also relished and been inspired by some outstanding cookbooks from Israeli food writers. However, as the book focuses on celebrating the unique attributes of the Palestinian kitchen, Israeli voices are not featured within these pages. This is not driven by any desire to exclude the Israeli experience, but only to create a space for the Palestinian experience to be explored.

———

The recipes here reflect the diversity of my travels. Some are classic dishes taught to me by Palestinian grandmothers; others are my interpretations of meals I ate in restaurants or at the homes of friends; others still are simply inspired by a local ingredient or technique. What unites them all is a celebration of the flavors rooted in the rich tradition of Palestinian cooking, in almost all cases brought together by *zaitoun* (the olive), the quintessential ingredient of the Palestinian kitchen that gave this book its name.

I hope you enjoy sharing this journey, and that the recipes bring you the same joy they brought me.

*Yasmin*
X

# A beginning

My plan was simple: I'd arrive in Tel Aviv late afternoon and jump straight on the train to Haifa to meet Raya, the Palestinian photographer who was accompanying me on my culinary journey and who had kindly offered to host me in her home.

We'd never met in person, but Raya's warmth and enthusiasm shone through on our Skype calls. What sealed the deal was when she showed me her latest tattoo, the stencilled outline of a halved pomegranate intertwined with vine leaves that runs up the back of her left calf. That's the photographer for me, I thought.

My plane landed from clear blue skies on a scorching July afternoon. Stepping onto the hot tarmac, my stomach rumbled as I pondered how to start my feasting. Perhaps a dish of braised okra, slow-cooked in a garlicky tomato sauce, or maybe cigarillos of chewy vine leaves, stuffed with spiced rice and lamb. If I was lucky, maybe a single diamond of flaky walnut baklava, syrup oozing from the sides.

But before then, I had to tackle the small issue of being a woman of Iranian-Pakistani heritage trying to enter Israel. Standing in line at immigration, I twiddled my silver Hamza necklace nervously, wondering if I should have taken it off. I'd been to Israel several times before, so I knew the drill. I'd be held for several hours, going back and forth between small interrogation rooms to be quizzed about every aspect of my past,

present and future. Israeli officials can force you to hand over email and social media login details as well as mobile phone passwords, and if, for whatever reason, they don't like the look of you, you're simply escorted onto a plane back to where you came from.

As I sat waiting for the first interrogation, my stomach rumbled again. I should have packed a sandwich, I thought. Rookie error. Over the next few hours, I was escorted to and from interrogations in which Israeli officials asked me a series of increasingly probing questions about my work, my family, my childhood, my health, my relationships and my political affiliations. It's a sophisticated system of questions designed to confuse and disorient, jumping from one subject to another and throwing so many repeating queries at you that your head starts throbbing. "Look," I said, exasperated and tired, "I'm just here doing research for a cookbook." My interrogator, who had not introduced himself in all the time we had spent together, fixed his smile, unwavering. "Do you know anyone in Hamas?" he replied.

———

Eventually, around nightfall, I was allowed through. My eyes were bloodshot, my nerves in shreds. Desperate to get out of the airport, I ignored the hunger pangs in my stomach and got right on the next train to Haifa. An hour later, I clambered out at Haifa-Carmel station. Raya was easy to spot with her broad smile and bright red hair pulled back from her face with a large hairclip, a few stray curls escaping to the

sides. We hugged each other like long-lost friends and spent the car journey back to her house ranting and laughing in equal measure at the ridiculousness of the situation, as she shared tale after tale of Palestinian friends who are routinely detained, strip-searched or made to miss flights. "They even took my camera once," she said sadly, staring at the road ahead.

———

We arrived at her apartment, with its encircling terrace. I walked out onto it, inhaling the dense, warm summer air, and peered into a courtyard surrounded by olive trees. I heard pots and pans clattering in the kitchen. Raya was making dinner. "Yasmin, do you like freekeh?" she called. Happily, I do.

She walked into the living room carrying a large serving dish, piled high with the nutty grains of smoked wheat, topped with thick slices of roasted squash and potatoes. The room filled with the soothing scent of allspice and nutmeg as she placed small bowls of yogurt and olives on the table to complete the meal. Each bite of the gently spiced, smoky freekeh comforted me and, by the last mouthful, the adrenaline that had pumped through my veins for hours began to wear off.

I yawned and glanced at the clock: 1.30am, time for bed. We moved the hand-stitched, Palestinian embroidered cushions off her Ikea sofa bed and I collapsed onto it, ready to put the day to bed. "Ahlan wa sahlan," said Raya as she turned off the light. Welcome to Palestine.

# Welcome to Palestine

Greetings are very important in Palestinian culture and if there is one phrase that you hear more than any other when traveling through Palestinian communities, it is this: *Ahlan wa sahlan.*

Usually loosely translated as 'welcome' in English, *Ahlan wa sahlan* also has a deeper meaning, representing something along the lines of, 'May you arrive as part of the family and tread an easy path as you enter.'

It is a phrase that is extended in greeting from falafel vendors and fruit sellers, *knafeh* makers and *khubz* bakers as Palestinians go out of their way to enthusiastically welcome guests from foreign lands. During a single day you're likely to hear it at least a dozen times, accompanied, always, by a beaming smile. The warmth with which Palestinians welcome strangers—and their passion for wanting to share immediately their food, drinks, homes and political opinions with you—is one the things I love most about traveling through the region.

It even extends to mobile phone providers and, upon arriving in the West Bank, I always break into a smile after hearing my mobile phone trill to announce a welcome text message. *'Marhaba,'* it reads (the universal Arabic phrase for 'hello'), *'Smell the jasmine and taste the olives. Jawwal welcomes you to Palestine.'* If there's a friendlier, more poetic way to be received into a country by a mobile phone provider anywhere in the world, I've yet to hear it.

———

This warmth and hospitality extends to the Palestinian kitchen and its food. Bursting with the freshness and brightness that are characteristic of all Levantine cooking, Palestinian food has evolved through the influences of Armenian, Bedouin, Jewish, Roman, Arabic, Persian and Turkish cultures, among those of the many other civilizations that have ruled over or lived in the area known as ancient Palestine for several millennia.

With a strong focus on local, plant-based food and seasonality, Palestinian cuisine is, for the most part, cooked simply and served unadorned, with fresh and cooked vegetables and pulses forming the bedrock of most meals.

There are three main regional varieties of Palestinian cuisine, each with its own unique take on spices, flavors, ingredients and cooking techniques.

The food of The Galilee has the most affinity with classic Levantine cooking as we know it—featuring a magnificent array of colorful *mazzeh* (mezze) dishes that make use of the region's bountiful eggplants, asparagus, peppers, artichokes and green beans—and specializes in *kibbeh*, a time-consuming, prized delicacy of pounded meatballs. The coastal towns of The Galilee also make judicious use of the fresh fish and seafood which is abundant on these warm Mediterranean shores.

Food from the West Bank focuses more on meat and bread, drawing its major influences from the cuisine of Jordan to the east and the Bedouin populations to the south. Famed dishes here include *mansaf*, a rich and hearty

lamb stew cooked in a sauce of fermented whey, or *mussakhan*, roast chicken seasoned with sumac and caramelized onions and served on *taboon* flatbreads.

The food of the Gaza Strip is the most distinct, using a flavor palette that embraces fresh dill, green chillies and copious amounts of garlic, and placing fish or seafood as the centerpiece for many meals. It is also, sadly, the cuisine that is under the biggest threat of disappearing, due to the crippling blockade which has plunged the Gaza Strip into devastating food poverty. Today, 80 percent of the 2 million inhabitants depend on UN food aid to survive, and Gaza's once strong fishing industry is in the process of being eradicated.

———

One of the most enduring aspects of Palestinian cuisine is its adaptability through all these challenges. Cuisine, like language, constantly evolves with the years, but, because of the constraints of the OPT, Palestinian food has undergone its own unique journey.

There are a few common principles, though. Yogurt is a staple and almost always present at dining tables in one form or another. It could be served as it is, to be spooned over dishes, or strained to make it thicker and firmer before being rolled into labneh balls, but either way it offers a cooling, refreshing buffer to the intense heat of the Palestinian summer.

Fresh salads of seasonal vegetables are a must and are eaten with every meal, and there are usually small bowls of pickles and olives, too, which bring the table together.

Domed round flatbreads, known as *khubz*, are essential for scooping up all the tasty morsels, and small bowls of extra virgin olive oil and za'atar often accompany them, the custom being to dip the bread first in oil and then in the spice mix.

Food is accompanied by fresh juices or water, and there is increasingly an exciting selection of artisan Palestinian beers, wines and arak to choose from. Caffeine comes mainly in the form of coffee—drunk in short, dark, strong and sweet shots flavored with cardamom—but black tea is also enjoyed, infused with fresh sage or mint leaves.

# The Palestinian store cupboard

What follows is an introduction to the vital ingredients you'll need to have in your kitchen before you tackle Palestinian recipes. First of all, though, a few words to help you cook the food in this book.

The importance placed on local produce and seasonality in Palestinian cuisine brings a refreshing flexibility to many of the recipes. You can easily substitute zucchini for eggplant, for instance, or squash for carrots, depending on which ingredients are available locally where you are in the world. So embrace the Palestinian style of cooking and eat with the seasons; your health, your wallet and the environment will thank you for it.

Many Palestinian dishes will succeed or fail depending on the quality of the olive oil that you use, so be sure to get the best you can afford for that final flourish. Palestinian olive oil is widely available in supermarkets and speciality stores and I recommend starting with that; it imparts a wondrous peppery note.

A final word on seasoning, which is often given in measured quantities in these recipes. Seasoning must always be adapted according to the ingredients you are using, to the accompanying dishes and to personal preference, so taste the recipes while you are cooking them and adjust the seasoning. Sometimes all it takes is a crumble of sea salt flakes, a generous grind of black pepper or a squeeze of lemon juice to elevate an average dish into an extraordinary meal.

## OLIVES AND OLIVE OIL

The olive—*zaitoun* in Arabic—is the most emblematic of all Palestinian ingredients and forms the bedrock of Palestinian cooking. Most dishes use olive oil as a form of seasoning and it's not uncommon for Palestinian households to have several different bottles on the go, with cooks swapping between them as needed. I highly recommend you do the same. Use extra virgin oil for finishing dishes and any neutral oil for cooking and baking. It is worth trying to track down Palestinian extra virgin olive oils, which are now available in many supermarkets or online: they are deeply pungent and aromatic, and their intensity makes them perfect for dressing salads, adding a finishing touch to soups, or as a dip for warm bread with za'atar. But, whatever you do, don't cook with them, as extra virgin olive oil has a low smoke point that, if reached, can reduce the nutritional benefits and may even produce harmful chemicals.

## BREAD

The essential component for any table, many Palestinians feel they haven't eaten unless they have had bread. Flatbreads are the most common form eaten in Palestinian kitchens and, nowadays, Arabic flatbreads (which have some affinity with naan breads) are readily available in most supermarkets. Stick them in the freezer and you'll always have some on hand for a Middle Eastern feast.

## BULGUR

A type of whole wheat grain that has been cracked and partially pre-cooked. Different sizes or grades of bulgur require varying cooking times, so it's always best to check the packet for cooking instructions. One huge advantage of using bulgur wheat is that, as it has already been partially cooked, it's much quicker to get on the table than many other whole grains and most types will be ready in just 15 minutes.

## FLOWER WATERS

Beautifully fragrant rose water and slightly bitter orange blossom water are used in sweet pastries and baked goods. A little can go a long way and each bottle will vary in strength, so it is best to add these powerful elixirs in stages and taste as you go along.

## FREEKEH

This is made from young wheat that has been roasted and then cracked to varying degrees of coarseness. The grains are pale green and have a similar texture to bulgur, but a far different taste, with wonderfully rich, nutty and smoky flavor notes and a definite bite. Freekeh is primarily used in soups, pilafs and salads.

## FRUIT (DRIED)

Dried figs and dates are the most common dried fruits used in Palestinian cuisine, often served up as a sweet treat alongside small cups of scented coffee or tea.

## FRUIT MOLASSES

The concentrated molasses of pomegranates, grapes and carob are all commonly used in Palestinian cuisine. Grape molasses and tahini are often paired together for a traditional Palestinian breakfast (if you can't find grape molasses, date molasses is a good substitute), while carob molasses is used to make sweet desserts such as the rich and creamy milk pudding known as *khabeeza*. All these products are readily available in health food shops, Middle Eastern stores or some larger supermarkets. Just one word of advice: when buying pomegranate molasses, check the label to make sure no extra sugar has been added; that way you can control the sweet and sharp balance of your dishes.

## MAFTOOL

Often referred to as a Palestinian couscous, *maftool* comprises hand-rolled balls of bulgur wheat that have also been rolled in flour. Unlike traditional couscous, *maftool* doesn't lose its shape while cooking, making it very forgiving to work with. *Maftool* works well as a substitute for rice or bulgur alongside any dish that has a sauce, and I often like to use it as a base for a salad, too, or as a side dish for platters of roasted meats, grilled fish or seafood.

## NUTS

Pine nuts are used to adorn many Palestinian dishes, giving a rich, buttery flavor and texture. A little toasting brings out their flavor, it just takes a minute and makes all the difference.

Do keep a close eye on the kernels while they toast, because they are so small and high in oil that they easily scorch. Their high oil content also causes them to turn rancid very quickly so, if possible, smell pine nuts before buying them, then store them in the fridge or freezer in a tightly sealed container. Almonds, walnuts and pistachios are also used in Palestinian cuisine, enjoyed as a snack, or eaten in desserts.

### PULSES

Chickpeas are the primary legumes enjoyed in Palestinian food, eaten in everything from hummus to pilafs to stews. I use canned and dried chickpeas—it is handy to have both in your store cupboard—alongside green, brown and red lentils; all are used to give heft to rice dishes, run through salads or make thick soups.

### RICE

A relative newcomer to Palestinian cuisine, rice isn't grown locally and, as an imported product, used only to be enjoyed by the rich, or eaten on special occasions. Over the last 50 years this has changed, and today rice has become commonplace, though Palestinian cooks tend to use a short-grain Egyptian variety. As this isn't easy to come by in the West, I stick to basmati rice in most of the recipes in this book.

### SPICES

The Palestinian kitchen uses small amounts of warming, sweet spices such as cinnamon, allspice, nutmeg, cumin, cilantro, coriander seeds, paprika, black pepper, cloves and cardamom. Spices are used judiciously, so as not to overpower the other ingredients and to allow the flavor of the meat or vegetables they are partnered with to sing through. Sumac is a popular spice, made from the dried and ground sumac berry. It is used to add astringency and sharpness to dishes and has an affinity with grilled meats and salads.

### YOGURT

A Palestinian staple, yogurt is eaten alongside most stews and grilled meat dishes and often strained to form a tangy thick spread known as labneh, traditionally eaten with bread and za'atar for breakfast.

### ZA'ATAR

The name for both a wild herb (a variety of thyme) that grows throughout the region and for the iconic Palestinian spice mix (in which the herb is mixed with sumac, sesame seeds and salt and used as a tangy condiment). I use za'atar for everything from marinating meats and fish to roasting vegetables. Look for brands that have been made in the Middle East, as many supermarket versions in the West tend to be dry, woody and tasteless.

# MAZZEH

Palestinians wholeheartedly embrace relaxed and informal eating, which is one of the many reasons that I adore Palestinian food.

It is quite common for half a dozen dishes to be dotted around the table and guests are simply invited to help themselves to as much or as little as they please. Many *mazzeh* dishes are best served at room temperature so can be made ahead, which is perfect for a home cook like me who doesn't like stressing in the kitchen, trying to get everything ready at the same time. It's also very handy if you are entertaining and want to get all the cooking done before your guests arrive.

English speakers will be familiar with the word *mezze*. The Palestinians equivalent is *mazzeh*, or even *muqabalat*, depending on regional dialect, or which community the speaker belongs to.

# Hummus

Let's start with the most iconic of all Palestinian dishes: thick bowls of hummus, drenched in tahini and singing with citrusy flavor. Palestinians mainly eat hummus for breakfast, when it is commonly topped with tangy chilli-and-lemon-dressed chickpeas (see page 26) and served with thick slices of tomatoes and crunchy wedges of cucumber. A lot has been written about The Perfect Hummus... but I'm not a purist. Lemon and garlic levels are a matter of taste, so, while I suggest amounts you might start with, I encourage you to adapt them as you like. As brands of tahini can vary, feel free to play with the quantities of that, too.

Here is a basic hummus, and on the following pages two more elaborate versions that elevate the simple chickpea to a more sophisticated main meal. Just be sure to process the chickpeas while they are still warm, to achieve the lightest, creamiest result.

**Serves 4–6 as part of a spread**

1 ¼ cups/250g dried chickpeas
1 teaspoon baking soda
3 garlic cloves, crushed
6 tablespoons/90ml lemon juice, or to taste
3 cups/180g tahini
½ teaspoon ground cumin
sea salt
4 ice cubes
extra virgin olive oil, to serve

OPTIONAL EXTRAS
pinch of za'atar, paprika or ground cumin

Soak the chickpeas overnight in a large bowl of cold water.

The next day, drain the chickpeas, tip them into a saucepan with the baking soda, cover with water and bring to a simmer. After 5 minutes of cooking, stir the chickpeas and skim off the foam that rises. Cook until the chickpeas are soft but not completely mushy. Depending on their freshness, this could take 30–40 minutes.

When they are ready, drain them and place the hot chickpeas in a food processor with the garlic, lemon juice, tahini, cumin and 1½ teaspoons salt. Process until the mixture is smooth, then add the ice cubes and process for another 2 full minutes, until the hummus looks light and creamy. Taste and adjust the seasoning, adding a touch more lemon juice or salt according to taste and splashing in a little cold water if it is looking a bit thick (it will thicken more upon cooling).

Transfer to a serving bowl and leave to rest for 1 hour for the flavors to come together.

To serve, use the back of a spoon to make a well in the hummus and drizzle over some extra virgin olive oil. You could also finish with a pinch of za'atar, paprika or ground cumin, if you like.

# Hummus with spiced lamb

HUMMUS QAWARMA

Discovering this spectacular combination of juicy marinated lamb spooned over velvety smooth hummus was one of the culinary highlights of my first visit to the West Bank. Incredibly simple to make, this winning combination has fast become one of my kitchen staples whenever I need a quick, nourishing dinner. I've written this recipe using a batch of home-made Hummus (see page 22) but, to be honest, you could spruce up shop-bought hummus with this delicious topping, too. Serve it with a bright, fresh salad and a bowl of crunchy Middle Eastern pickles. Use ground lamb instead of fillet if you like but, if you do, leave out the extra virgin olive oil from the marinade.

**Serves 4 as a main dish, or 6 as part of a spread**

FOR THE LAMB AND MARINADE
12 oz./300g lamb neck or loin fillet
1 garlic clove, crushed
2 tablespoons lemon juice
1 tablespoon extra virgin olive oil, plus more to serve (optional)
1/2 teaspoon sumac
1/2 teaspoon dried oregano
1/4 teaspoon ground turmeric
pinch of Aleppo pepper (*pul biber*), or cayenne pepper
sea salt and freshly ground black pepper
2 tablespoons light olive oil, to fry

FOR THE REST
1/4 cup/30g pine nuts
1 recipe Hummus (see page 22)
small handful of chopped parsley leaves
sumac

Chop the lamb fillet into 1cm-thick pieces. Mix in all the marinade ingredients except the light olive oil, seasoning with 1/2 teaspoon salt and 1/4 teaspoon pepper, and ensure that the lamb is fully coated. Cover and leave to marinate for at least 30 minutes or up to 1 hour.

Heat the light olive oil in a frying pan and fry the meat for 3–4 minutes over a medium heat until it is just cooked through.

Toast the pine nuts by placing them in a small dry pan over a medium heat and stirring them for a minute or so until they turn golden brown. Set them aside in a small bowl.

When you are ready to eat, transfer the hummus to a couple of serving bowls and use the back of a spoon to make a shallow well in each. Spoon the lamb over, finishing with a sprinkling of parsley, the toasted pine nuts and a pinch of sumac. Drizzle with a little extra virgin olive oil, if you like.

LEFT: Hummus with spiced lamb.
FAR LEFT: Hummus with lemon and green chilli chickpeas (see next page).

# Hummus with lemon and green chilli chickpeas

HUMMUS MUSABAHA

Sharp and tangy with a gentle green chilli kick, this traditional Palestinian breakfast dish is one of the best ways you can start your day. Serve it with falafel and pickles for a moreish weekend brunch, or as part of a spread.

Serves 4–6 as part of a spread

**FOR THE HUMMUS**
1 1/4 cups/250g dried chickpeas
1 teaspoon baking soda
1 1/2 garlic cloves, crushed
3 tablespoons lemon juice, or to taste
1 1/2 cups/90g tahini
1/4 teaspoon ground cumin
sea salt
2 ice cubes

**FOR THE TOPPING**
1 garlic clove, crushed
1 small green chilli, finely chopped, deseeded if you prefer
4 tablespoons/10g parsley leaves, finely chopped
4 tablespoons lemon juice
4 tablespoons extra virgin olive oil, plus more to serve
freshly ground black pepper

Soak the chickpeas overnight and cook them with the baking soda as on page 22, reserving 1/2 cup (about 100ml) of their cooking liquid.

When they are ready, drain them and place half the hot chickpeas in a food processor with the garlic, lemon juice, tahini, cumin and 3/4 teaspoon salt. Cover the remaining chickpeas and set aside. Process until the mixture is smooth, then add the ice cubes and process for another 2 full minutes, until the hummus looks light and creamy. Taste and adjust the seasoning, adding a touch more lemon juice or salt according to taste and splashing in a little cold water if it is a bit thick (it will thicken upon cooling).

Transfer to a serving bowl and leave to rest for 1 hour for the flavors to come together.

Dress the remaining whole chickpeas with all the topping ingredients, seasoning with 3/4 teaspoon salt and 1/4 teaspoon pepper and mixing well. When you are ready to eat, transfer the hummus to a couple of plates and use the back of a spoon to make a shallow well in each. Spoon the chickpea mixture over them and finish with a good drizzle of extra virgin olive oil.

# Fava bean and dill dip

This flavorsome summer dish improves with time, so is a great make-ahead number. Fava beans and dill are a magical pairing and here they are mixed with sweet, tender peas and tangy sumac for an addictive companion to flatbread or crudités. You can use fresh or frozen beans and peas, you'll just need to adjust the cooking time slightly.

**Serves 2–3 as a main dish, or 4–6 as part of a spread**

16 oz./500g fresh or frozen
  fava beans (podded weight)
1 cup/150g peas
juice of 1 lemon, or to taste
1 garlic clove, crushed
1/4 cup/60g Greek yogurt
1/2 teaspoon sumac,
  plus more to serve

2 tablespoons chopped dill
small handful of mint leaves,
  plus more to serve
1 teaspoon dried mint
sea salt and freshly ground
  black pepper
extra virgin olive oil

Bring a saucepan of water to the boil. Add the fava beans and cook until soft (depending whether they are fresh or frozen this will take 2–4 minutes). Add the peas when the fava beans are almost ready; they only need to be in the pan for a short time. When both the vegetables are tender, drain and rinse under cold water.

Peel the fava beans, popping them out of their dull green skins one by one, then place in a food processor with the peas, lemon juice, garlic, yogurt, sumac, dill and fresh and dried mint. Add 3/4 teaspoon salt, 1/2 teaspoon pepper and 2 tablespoons extra virgin olive oil and blitz until the mixture is smooth.

Taste and adjust the seasoning, adding an extra squeeze of lemon juice or some more salt and pepper if needed.

To serve, scatter with a couple of extra mint leaves, a pinch of sumac and a generous drizzle of extra virgin olive oil.

# Charred eggplant with tahini

MUTABAL

Smoke-scented eggplant dip is a classic of Levantine cuisine. Key to imparting the essential smoky flavor is to cook the eggplants until their skins have completely blackened. This is best achieved over a barbecue, but I find that grilling them on the highest setting your oven can manage also gives good results. Just be sure to pierce each eggplant with a fork a few times before they go under the grill, or there is a risk that they might explode.

**Serves 4–6 as part of a spread**

3 lb./1.5kg eggplants (around 5 large ones)
2 garlic cloves, crushed
4 tablespoons tahini
juice of 1 lemon, or to taste

sea salt and freshly ground black pepper
1 tablespoon extra virgin olive oil, plus more to serve
finely chopped parsley leaves

Heat your grill to its highest setting and turn on the exhaust fan. Pierce the eggplants a few times with a fork, place them on a baking sheet and grill for 45–60 minutes, turning them a few times, until the skins have completely blackened and they have collapsed and are soft inside.

When the eggplants are cooked, take them out of the oven and run a knife lengthways through each one to open them and help to cool them down. Once they have cooled, scoop out their flesh and roughly chop it. Place the eggplant in a bowl with the garlic, tahini, lemon juice, 3/4 teaspoon salt, 1/4 teaspoon pepper and the extra virgin olive oil. Stir well, cover and leave for at least 1 hour for the flavors to come together.

When you are ready to serve the *mutabal*, taste and adjust the seasoning with a little lemon juice or salt if you like, then finish with a sprinkle of parsley and a trickle of extra virgin olive oil.

# Labneh 3 ways

The summer months can be blisteringly hot in the Middle East, so it's no coincidence that all the countries of the region have a special affinity with cooling yogurt dishes that soothe the body. This tangy, strained labneh has the consistency of a cream cheese. It is a regular addition to Palestinian *mazzeh* (mezze) spreads, and often enjoyed at breakfast time. Making it is remarkably straightforward. Simply stir salt into Greek yogurt, place it in a cheesecloth and let time do the work. During a nice long wait, the whey strains out, leaving thick, concentrated labneh. Just sprinkle on a chosen topping (see opposite) and have a couple of warm flatbreads ready (see pages 38–41 for home-made). Start this at least 12 hours before you want to serve it, to allow it to drain. You will need a cheesecloth.

**Makes about 21 oz./600g**

3¹/₂ cups/1kg Greek yogurt      ³/₄ teaspoon sea salt

Mix the yogurt and salt, spoon into a cheesecloth, then fold the cloth in, drawing the sides together to make a pouch. Tie it to the tap over the kitchen sink and leave to drain overnight.

The next morning, check the consistency. After 12 hours, it will have thickened into regular labneh. If you want to thicken it further so you can roll it into balls, tie the cloth up, place in a sieve over a bowl and transfer to the fridge for another 12 hours.

## Olive oil and za'atar

This is the classic way to eat labneh as part of a Palestinian meal. Either place regular labneh in a small serving bowl, use the back of a spoon to make a small well in the middle, then fill it with 1 tablespoon za'atar and a drizzle of extra virgin olive oil, or roll firm, well-strained labneh into 1 in./2.5cm balls, coat with za'atar and drizzle with extra virgin olive oil.

## Peach, thyme and pistachio

For a sweeter breakfast or brunch dish, try serving labneh with honey-roasted stone fruits, such as peaches, apricots or nectarines. Preheat the oven to 350°F/180°C. Take a ripe peach, cut it into 3/4 in./2cm-thick wedges and place on a baking sheet. Drizzle over 2 teaspoons runny honey and sprinkle on 1 teaspoon thyme leaves, adding some sprigs of thyme if you like, then roast for 10 minutes. (You can also sear the peach slices on a very hot grill pan, adding the thyme and honey right at the end.) Place a few heaped tablespoons of regular labneh in a serving bowl, top with slices of roast or grilled peach, drizzle over more honey and finish with a smattering of chopped unsalted pistachios.

## Dukkah and olive oil

Best for lunch or evening meals, when you want a more robust flavor. Make Dukkah (see page 36). Place regular labneh in a small serving bowl, use a spoon to make a small well in the middle, then fill with 2 tablespoons dukkah and a drizzle of extra virgin olive oil.

**Pictured on next page**

# Olive, fig and honey tapenade

This recipe was inspired by a visit to the Canaan Fair Trade food co-operative in the north of the West Bank. The company produces artisan Palestinian foods that celebrate the region's agriculture. It works with local olive, nut and fig producers as well as with producers who forage more unusual wild-harvested ingredients such as capers. I've brought all these together in a sweet and salty Palestinian tapenade, which is exquisite on warm flatbreads.

**Serves 4–6 as part of a spread**

3/4 cup/100g pitted black olives
1/3 cup/40g walnuts
1 tablespoon capers, rinsed and drained
3 dried figs, stalks removed

2 teaspoons honey
3 tablespoons extra virgin olive oil
1/2 teaspoon apple cider vinegar

Place all the ingredients in a mini food processor and blend until they form a rough paste; don't over-blend, as the paste should retain some texture.

Leave for 1 hour before serving, for the flavors to come together.

# "Almost za'atar"

Za'atar is a wild herb, *Origanum syriacum*, that grows throughout the Levant. It's also the name of a common spice mix used as a marinade or dip. It's hard to replicate za'atar without herbs from the region and these days you can find it in supermarkets or online, but if you really can't find any on sale, this is a close approximation.

**Makes about 4 oz./100g**

2 tablespoons dried oregano
  (Greek or Turkish)
2 tablespoons dried
  marjoram
2 tablespoons sumac
2 teaspoons sesame seeds
1 teaspoon sea salt

Simply mix the ingredients together, then store in an airtight container for up to 2 weeks.

# Dukkah

This nut, seed and spice mix is used as a dip for bread. To eat it, tear off a chunk of bread and dunk it first in extra virgin olive oil and then in dukkah. You can also use the mixture as a seasoning for roast fish, meat or root vegetables. I make it in small batches of this size, so the spices remain fresh and the nuts crisp.

**Serves 6-8**

1/3 cup/40g almonds
1/2 cup/50g walnuts
2 tablespoons sesame seeds
1 tablespoon coriander seeds
1 tablespoon cumin seeds
generous pinch of
  ground allspice
1/2 teaspoon sea salt
1/4 teaspoon freshly
  ground black pepper

Place the nuts and seeds in a large pan, set over a medium heat and toast for 1 minute, or until the aromas are released and the nuts start to turn glossy. Remove from the heat and stir in the allspice, salt and pepper. Store in an airtight container for up to 1 week.

# Flatbreads with za'atar

MANA'EESH

These tangy flatbreads are the number one snack food in Palestine, you can buy them throughout the day from bakeries and street stalls in all the main cities. Adding yogurt to the dough keeps the bread lovely and soft and gives it a texture somewhat akin to that of naan bread. For making these flatbreads in domestic ovens—rather than the clay, fire-powered *taboon* ovens used in Palestinian cooking—I highly recommend using a pizza stone, as they get much hotter than a baking sheet. They aren't expensive to buy and are worth the investment.

Makes 8

2 cups/300g all-purpose flour, sifted, plus more to dust
1 tablespoon active dry yeast
1/2 teaspoon sea salt
1/2 teaspoon sugar
about 2/3 cup/150g unflavored yogurt
extra virgin olive oil
1/3 cup/75ml lukewarm water
5 tablespoons za'atar

Place the flour, yeast, salt and sugar in the bowl of an electric mixer fitted with a dough hook, or, if you are kneading by hand, simply place the ingredients in a large bowl.

Separately, whisk together the yogurt and 3 tablespoons extra virgin olive oil, then add to the flour, along with half the water.

Knead the dough for about 5 minutes on a medium setting in a mixer (or for 10 minutes by hand) until it has come together and is smooth, silky and pliable. If it looks a little dry, you can add the remaining water a little at a time.

There are a few different ways to tell if your dough is ready. You can give the ball of dough a firm poke with your finger and, if the indentation that you make fills quickly, you know it's done. If the dent stays, then continue kneading. In addition, I often do the "windowpane test," which involves taking a small piece of dough from the ball and stretching it between my fingers and thumbs into a very thin, almost translucent, square (so it looks a bit like a windowpane). If you can stretch the dough nice and thin without it breaking, then it's ready. If not, keep kneading it for a few more minutes.

When the dough has been well kneaded, use your fingertips to smooth its surface with a drop of olive oil, trying to very lightly coat it. Place in a large bowl, cover with plastic wrap and leave to rise in a warm place for about 1 hour, or until doubled in size.

Knock the air out of the dough by firmly whacking it on your work top a few times, then cut it into 8 equal-sized pieces. Using a rolling pin, roll each piece into a disc about ¼ inch/5mm thick. Cover with a clean, damp dish towel and leave to rise for 15 minutes.

Meanwhile, preheat the oven to its highest setting. Lightly dust a pizza stone or 2 baking sheets with a little flour (this will stop the bread from sticking) and place in the oven to heat up.

When you are ready to cook the *mana'eesh*, make the topping by mixing the za'atar and 5 tablespoons extra virgin olive oil in a small bowl. Brush this thick paste over the flatbreads.

Place the flatbreads on the hot stone or sheets; you will probably have to cook them in batches. Cook for about 3 minutes, until they start to puff up, then remove from the oven while you cook the rest. You can serve these immediately, or wait until they have cooled. They will keep for about 24 hours.

**Pictured on page 37**

# Arabic flatbreads

KHUBZ

These soft, chewy flatbreads are used as a utensil at the Palestinian table, where they are put to good use scooping up the vast array of tantalising small dishes and dips. I advise baking these on a pizza stone, as it will immensely improve the quality of the breads.

**Makes 6**

2 cups/250g bread flour, plus more to dust
2 teaspoons active dry yeast
1/4 teaspoon sugar
1 teaspoon sea salt
2/3 cup/160ml lukewarm water
1 tablespoon extra virgin olive oil, plus more for oiling the dough

If you are using an electric mixer fitted with a dough hook, place the flour, yeast, sugar and salt in its mixing bowl. Add half the water and the extra virgin olive oil. Knead for 5 minutes on a medium setting, or until the dough comes together in a ball. Every minute after this, gradually add a little of the remaining water, until all the flour has come away from the sides and you have a soft dough. (You may not need all the water.)

If kneading by hand, follow the process above but, once you have mixed all the ingredients together in a bowl, place the dough on a lightly floured surface and knead for 7–10 minutes. The dough will be wet in the beginning, but keep going and it will become smooth, stretchy and pliable.

There are a few different ways to tell if your dough is ready. You can give the ball of dough a firm poke with your finger and, if the indentation that you make fills quickly, you know it's done. If the dent stays, then continue kneading. In addition, I often do the "windowpane test," which involves taking a small piece of dough from the ball and stretching it between my fingers and thumbs into a very thin, almost translucent, square (so it looks a bit like a windowpane). If you can stretch the dough nice and thin without it breaking, then it's ready. If not, keep kneading it for a few more minutes.

When the dough has been well kneaded, use your fingertips to smooth its surface with a drop of olive oil, trying to very lightly coat it. Place in a large bowl, cover with plastic wrap and leave to rise in a warm place for about 1 hour, or until doubled in size.

Continued on next page

Knock the air out of the dough by firmly whacking it on your work top a few times. Cut it into 6 equal-sized balls. Using a rolling pin, roll each piece of dough into an oval about ¼ in./5mm thick. Cover with a clean, damp dish towel and leave to rise for a final 15 minutes.

Meanwhile, preheat the oven to its highest setting. Lightly dust a pizza stone or 2 baking sheets with a little flour (this will stop the bread from sticking) and place in the oven to heat up.

Place the flatbreads on the hot stone or sheets; you will probably have to cook them in batches. Cook for 3–5 minutes, until the breads have just puffed up and are starting to color. Remove from the oven and cover with a clean cloth until cool, while you cook the remaining breads. Serve as soon as possible, or at least within a few hours.

# Herbed focaccia

There is nothing quite like tearing apart a big loaf of bread at a shared dining table, and this recipe is inspired by a meal I shared with graphic designer Haitham Haddad at Rai's café in Haifa, which serves some of the best focaccia I've ever tasted (see page 68). It is an extremely forgiving loaf to make and a great one to start with if you are new to baking. Serve it with small bowls of extra virgin olive oil, za'atar and dukkah (see page 36 for home-made) on the side, into which you can dunk your bread. Thick wedges of fried eggplant, sliced tomatoes and some labneh (see page 30) would transform this into a classic Palestinian breakfast.

**Makes 1 large loaf**

3½ cups/500g bread flour
2½ teaspoons sea salt
2½ teaspoons sugar
¼ oz./7g active dry yeast
2 tablespoons olive oil, plus more for handling the dough
1¾ cups/400ml lukewarm water

FOR THE TOPPING
2 tablespoons olive oil
½ red onion, finely sliced
½ tablespoon za'atar
sea salt and freshly ground black pepper

Place the flour, salt, sugar, yeast, 2 tablespoons olive oil and 1¼ cups/300ml of the water into a large bowl. Bring the mixture together with your hands to form a dough, then either knead the dough in an electric mixer fitted with a dough hook on a medium speed for 5 minutes, or knead it by hand for 10 minutes on an oiled surface. Gradually add the remaining water as you knead.

Place the dough in a large bowl, cover with plastic wrap or a clean, damp dish towel and leave to rise in a warm place until doubled in size (this should take about 1 hour).

Tip the dough out of the bowl and onto a large baking sheet. You don't need to knock the air out as you would with other breads, simply flatten and stretch the dough into an oval shape, then cover and leave it to rise for another hour.

Preheat the oven to 425°F/220°C. Place a pizza stone or an upside-down baking sheet in the oven to warm up for 10 minutes.

Now for the topping. Brush the loaf with the olive oil, add the sliced onion, then sprinkle over the za'atar and some salt and pepper. Use your fingers to poke dimples into the top of the focaccia, then place it, still on its sheet, on the hot pizza stone or baking sheet in the oven and bake for 20–25 minutes, until golden brown on top.

# Roast red peppers
# with olives and capers

Wild capers grow throughout the Palestinian territories and in recent years there has been a resurgence, driven by Palestinian chefs, to encourage the use of them. I've taken their lead with this dish, which is inspired by my travels around the north of the West Bank, where I found local food co-operatives selling locally grown sun-dried tomatoes, olives and capers. These elements come together in a quick and flavorsome stuffing for roast red peppers.

**Serves 4 as part of a spread, or as a side dish**

4 red peppers
2 garlic cloves, finely sliced
4 medium tomatoes, finely chopped
2 tablespoons capers, rinsed and drained
¼ cup/30g pitted black olives, roughly chopped

2 tablespoons za'atar (or substitute 1½ tablespoons dried oregano plus ½ teaspoon sumac)
2 tablespoons apple cider vinegar
4 tablespoons extra virgin olive oil
sea salt and freshly ground black pepper

Preheat the oven to 400°F/200°C.

Cut the peppers in half, trim off any white pith and place them in a baking sheet.

Mix the garlic, tomatoes, capers, olives, za'atar, vinegar and extra virgin olive oil together. Season with 1 teaspoon salt and ½ teaspoon pepper.

Stuff each pepper with a few spoonfuls of the filling, then cover the sheet with foil.

Bake for 20 minutes, then remove the foil and bake for another 20–30 minutes, until the peppers are completely soft and a little darkened around the edges.

# Roast okra with spicy tomatoes

BAMIYEH

When cooked just right, the plump, tender seed pods of the okra plant are my idea of food heaven. Their flavor is somewhere between asparagus and eggplant and their soft texture is perfect for squashing between warm flatbreads. To avoid any unwanted gloopiness—which has, regrettably, unfairly come to tarnish this handsome fruit's reputation—be sure not to trim the stalks too close to the head, so they remained sealed. And yes, even though we refer to it and use it as a vegetable, technically it is a fruit.

**Serves 4–6 as part of a spread**

1 lb./500g okra
4 tablespoons olive oil or any neutral oil
sea salt and freshly ground black pepper
1 onion, finely sliced
1/2 teaspoon coriander seeds
1/2 teaspoon cumin seeds
1/4 teaspoon ground allspice
3 garlic cloves, finely sliced
1/4 teaspoon chilli flakes
14 oz./400g can of plum tomatoes
2 teaspoons superfine sugar
1 tablespoon lemon juice
extra virgin olive oil, to serve

Preheat the oven to 400°F/200°C.

Trim the okra by cutting off the stalks, but do so carefully by not slicing too close to the main pod: you want to keep each pod sealed so the seeds don't spill out, as this way the okra will remain firm while cooking.

Place the okra on a large baking sheet, drizzle over 2 tablespoons cooking oil and season well with salt and pepper. Roast for 15–20 minutes until the okra is tender but still firm.

Meanwhile, make the tomato sauce. Place the remaining 2 tablespoons cooking oil in a frying pan and gently fry the onion over a medium heat for 10 minutes, until it is soft.

Toast the coriander and cumin seeds by placing them in a dry pan over a low heat and stirring for a minute or so, until their aromas are released. Then crush in a mortar and pestle or spice grinder and add them to the onion with the allspice, garlic and chilli flakes. Fry for 2 minutes.

Add the tomatoes, sugar, lemon juice, 3/4 teaspoon salt and 1/2 teaspoon pepper. Cover and simmer for 10 minutes. Once the okra is out of the oven, add it to the tomato sauce and cook for a further 5 minutes, splashing in a little hot water if the sauce looks a bit dry. Taste, adjust the seasoning and drizzle with a generous glug of extra virgin olive oil just before serving.

# Shakshuka

This is a dish that transports me straight to the warm, balmy evenings I spent in Haifa with my photographer, Raya Manaa'. Most evenings we would get back to her apartment exhausted from a long day of travel and I'd promptly collapse on the sofa as she somehow found the energy to throw together one amazing dish after another. This was one of my favorites: soft, creamy eggs shaken in a rich tomato sauce that we scooped up with warm breads as we sat on her balcony under the olive trees and jasmine flowers. An utterly simple yet completely satisfying supper. I've suggested using canned tomatoes here, but if you are more blessed than me and live in warmer climes where shop-bought tomatoes are flavorsome, then instead skin 5–6 ripe ones after blanching them in just-boiled water, then coarsely grate them.

**Serves 2 as part of a spread**

3 tablespoons olive oil or any neutral oil
1 small red onion, finely chopped
2 garlic cloves, crushed
1/2 teaspoon paprika, plus more to serve
1/4 teaspoon ground allspice
1/4 teaspoon ground cumin
pinch of cayenne pepper
14 oz./400g can of plum tomatoes
1 teaspoon sugar
sea salt and freshly ground black pepper
4 eggs
small handful of cilantro, roughly chopped
extra virgin olive oil

Heat the cooking oil in a saucepan that has a lid and fry the onion for about 10 minutes, until soft. Stir in the garlic and spices and cook for another couple of minutes.

Pour in the tomatoes, sugar and 1/2 teaspoon salt. Cover and simmer for 15 minutes over a medium heat. Taste and adjust the seasoning.

Make 4 small wells in the sauce with the back of a spoon and gently break an egg into each of them. Season lightly, then reduce the heat, cover and cook for about 5 minutes, until just set. Halfway through cooking, run a spoon through the yolks so they break slightly. Sprinkle with the chopped cilantro and a smidgen more paprika and serve immediately, drizzled with extra virgin olive oil.

# Lemon and chilli roast potatoes

BATATA HARRA

These delectable bites of crispy roast potatoes doused with lemon juice, olive oil and warming chilli are one of the most welcome additions to any *mazzeh* (mezze) spread. Originating from the culinary traditions of The Galilee, they are a fun and easy way to spruce up the humble spud.

**Serves 4–6 as part of a spread**

4 tablespoons olive oil or any neutral oil
2 lb./1kg potatoes
sea salt and freshly ground black pepper
5 garlic cloves, crushed
1 tablespoon Aleppo pepper (*pul biber*) or half that amount of chilli flakes
½ teaspoon paprika
juice of ½ lemon
extra virgin olive oil
finely chopped cilantro, to serve

Preheat the oven to 400°F/200°C. Pour the cooking oil into a large baking pan and place in the oven to heat up.

Peel the potatoes and cut them into ¾ in./2cm cubes. Add them to a saucepan of boiling water with 2 teaspoons salt and cook for 5 minutes. Drain.

Take the pan out of the oven and add the potatoes with the garlic, Aleppo pepper, paprika, 1 teaspoon salt and ½ teaspoon pepper. Toss everything together quickly, then return the pan to the oven and bake for about 30 minutes, or until the potatoes are cooked through.

As soon as you take the potatoes out of the oven, judiciously squeeze the lemon juice all over them and stir well. Taste and adjust the seasoning, then transfer to a warmed serving plate, drizzle over a splash of extra virgin olive oil and add a scattering of cilantro.

# Green beans with olive oil

FASOLIA BI ZAIT

Palestinian home cooking celebrates the simple treatment of seasonal ingredients and this recipe is one of its greatest treasures. Firm and juicy green beans are served with a rich, garlicky tomato sauce and then smothered in olive oil (*bi zait* means 'in oil'), in a dish that is one of the staples of the region. As with many Palestinian dishes, you can serve this warm or at room temperature for a fresh-but-filling side dish.

**Serves 4 as part of a spread**

2 tablespoons olive oil or any neutral oil
2 onions, finely chopped
4 garlic cloves, finely sliced
3/4 teaspoon ground cumin
1/2 teaspoon ground allspice
14 oz./400g can of plum tomatoes
1 teaspoon sugar
sea salt and freshly ground black pepper
12 oz./350g green beans, trimmed
extra virgin olive oil

Pour the cooking oil into a frying pan and gently fry the onions over a medium heat for 15 minutes, until they are soft and translucent. Add the garlic and spices and cook for another few minutes.

Add the tomatoes, sugar, 3/4 teaspoon salt and a generous grind of pepper. Cover and leave to simmer for 10 minutes, adding a little hot water if the pan starts to look dry.

Meanwhile, boil the green beans in a saucepan of water until they are just cooked through but still have some bite. Drain, then add them to the tomato sauce.

Taste and adjust the seasoning, then drizzle with a couple of tablespoons of extra virgin olive oil just before serving.

# Seared halloumi with orange, dates and pomegranate

This delightful recipe is a ray of sunshine on a plate, transporting you to the warm shores of the Mediterranean with its great, refreshing combination of sharp citrus, tangy pomegranate seeds and sweet dates. I love to serve it with toasted flatbreads for a cheerful weekend brunch.

**Serves 4 as part of a spread**

8 oz./250g halloumi cheese
1 orange
1 tablespoon olive oil or any neutral oil (optional)
2 oz./50g Medjool dates, pitted and finely sliced
2 tablespoons pomegranate seeds
2 tablespoons extra virgin olive oil
1 tablespoon unsweetened pomegranate molasses
small handful of mint leaves, finely chopped

Slice the halloumi into ¼ in./1cm-thick slices.

Remove the segments from the orange: slice the top and bottom off the fruit, cutting deep enough that you see a wheel of orange flesh on both sides. Place the fruit on one of its flat ends, then slice off the remaining peel and pith, following the contour of the fruit. To remove individual segments, insert your knife as close as you can to the inside membrane of each segment and cut to the core. Do this on both sides of the segment; it should release with no pith.

Heat a large frying pan over a medium heat. Add the cooking oil if you need to; this will depend on the quality of your pan. Cook the halloumi on both sides until golden brown, then transfer to a serving plate.

Scatter the orange segments, dates and pomegranate seeds over the warm cheese. Mix the extra virgin olive oil and pomegranate molasses in a small bowl and drizzle this over before finishing with a smattering of mint. Serve immediately.

# Gazan smashed avocados

Avocados grow throughout the Gaza Strip and in this recipe they are paired with garlic and green chilli for a spicy side dish. Use the ripest avocados you can find here, as those will give the creamiest results. When Ahmed made this for me (see page 164), he called it the "Gazan guac," and—like that South American namesake—it makes an excellent dip.

**Serves 4 as part of a spread**

2 Hass avocados
1 garlic clove, crushed
1 green chilli, finely chopped
juice of ½ lemon, or to taste
2 tablespoons Greek yogurt or labneh (see page 30 for home-made)

2 tablespoons extra virgin olive oil, plus more to serve
sea salt and freshly ground black pepper
1 teaspoon sesame seeds
sumac, to serve

Halve the avocados lengthways, remove the pits, then spoon the insides into a bowl and mash them with a fork. You want a bit of texture, so don't feel the need to get it completely smooth.

Add the rest of the ingredients, except the sesame seeds and sumac, seasoning with ¾ teaspoon salt and ½ teaspoon pepper and stirring well. Taste and adjust the seasoning, adding a touch more lemon juice or salt as you prefer, then sprinkle with the sesame seeds and sumac and drizzle with extra virgin olive oil. Serve immediately.

# Asparagus with eggs and za'atar

HALAYONE W BAYD

This recipe is inspired by my conversations with Vivien Sansour, a botanist extraordinaire who is on a mission to save Palestinian heirloom seeds (see page 201). Wild asparagus is one of Vivien's favorite vegetables. She often makes a version of this dish in her mobile kitchen, in which she travels around the West Bank, speaking to farmers about the importance of conserving seeds. The quality of the za'atar is paramount here, so I recommend buying a Middle Eastern brand.

**Serves 4-6 as part of a spread**

2 tablespoons olive oil or any neutral oil
2 banana shallots (about 2 oz./70g total prepared weight), finely chopped
1 garlic clove, crushed
8 oz./250g asparagus, chopped into ¾ in./2cm pieces
sea salt and freshly ground black pepper
5 eggs
2 teaspoons za'atar
extra virgin olive oil

Heat the cooking oil in a frying or sauté pan. Add the shallots and fry for around 10 minutes until they are soft, then add the garlic and fry for another few minutes.

Add the chopped asparagus and season with ½ teaspoon each salt and pepper. Cover and cook over a medium heat until the asparagus pieces are just softened but still have some bite; this should take around 5 minutes depending on their size, age and variety. Keep an eye on them so you can judge when they are cooked to your liking.

Whisk the eggs in a bowl with a small pinch of salt and pour them over the asparagus. Using a wooden spoon, gently scramble the eggs around the asparagus, taking them off the heat just before they are set, so they don't overcook.

Transfer to a warmed serving plate and finish with a light dredging of za'atar and a good drizzle of extra virgin olive oil.

# Spinach and feta parcels

FATAYER SABANEKH

These dainty little pockets of stuffed pastry are an everyday Palestinian snack. I learned how to make them in the kitchen of Naya Manaa', a secretary from the Palestinian village of Majd al-Krum, who gave me the tip of using yogurt to enrich the dough, which also stops them from drying out. You can make the *fatayer* with a variety of seasonal leaves, such as Swiss chard or spring greens, just be sure to get them as dry as possible in the initial cooking stages, as if they are too wet they will create steam, which could push the pastry seams open. These parcels make perfect picnic food and keep well in an airtight container for 2–3 days.

**Makes 16**

**FOR THE PASTRY**
2½ cups/300g all-purpose flour, sifted
1 tablespoon active dry yeast
½ teaspoon sea salt
½ teaspoon sugar
about ⅔ cup/150g unflavored yogurt
3 tablespoons extra virgin olive oil, plus more for oiling the dough
about 2 tablespoons lukewarm water (optional)
1 egg (optional)

**FOR THE FILLING**
2 lb./900g fresh spinach or Swiss chard leaves, roughly chopped
2 scallions, finely chopped
2 oz./60g feta cheese, crumbled
2 tablespoons sumac
generous grind of nutmeg
2 tablespoons extra virgin olive oil
3 tablespoons pine nuts
sea salt and freshly ground black pepper

To make the pastry, place the flour, yeast, salt and sugar in a large bowl. Separately whisk together the yogurt and extra virgin olive oil, then add to the dry ingredients.

Knead the dough in an electric mixer fitted with a dough hook for 6–8 minutes on a medium setting, or for 10–15 minutes by hand, until it comes together and is smooth, silky and pliable. As you are kneading you can add a touch of the water, a little at a time, if the dough looks a little dry.

There are a few different ways to tell if your dough is ready. You can give the ball of dough a firm poke with your finger and, if the indentation that you make fills quickly, you know it's done. If the dent stays, then continue kneading. In addition, I often do the "windowpane test," which involves taking a small piece of dough from the ball and stretching it between my fingers and thumbs into a very thin, almost translucent, square (so it looks a bit like a windowpane). If you can stretch the dough nice and thin without it breaking, then it's ready. If not, keep kneading it for a few more minutes.

Continued on page 60

When the dough is ready, pop it into a large bowl and use your fingertips to smooth its surface with a drop of olive oil. Cover with plastic wrap and leave to rise in a warm place for 1 hour, or until doubled in size.

Knock the air out of the risen dough by whacking it on your work top a few times. Cut it into 16 equal-sized pieces and roll each into a disc about ¼ in./5mm thick and 4 in./10cm wide. Line 2 baking sheets with parchment paper, place the discs on them, cover with a clean, damp dish towel and leave to rise for a final 15 minutes.

Now make the filling. Cook the spinach (or chard) in a large saucepan over a medium heat for 5-7 minutes, stirring every so often to stop it sticking, until it darkens and most of its water has evaporated. Place it in a colander and, when cool enough to handle, squeeze as much water from it as possible. The drier you can get the cooked leaves, the better (see recipe introduction).

Place the leaves in a large bowl and add all the other filling ingredients, with 1 teaspoon salt and ¼ teaspoon pepper.

Preheat the oven to 400°F/200°C.

Spoon about 1½ tablespoons of the filling mixture into the center of each pastry disc. Then mold the pastry into a triangle shape by pulling 3 sides of it up and over the filling and into the middle. Press the pastry edges together to seal the triangle. Score each parcel with a fork in a couple of places and then brush with a little olive oil. (You can also use an egg wash here, made by whisking 1 egg with 1 tablespoon water and brushing it over the pastry. This isn't strictly necessary, but will help the dough to bind together at the seams.) Return to the prepared baking sheets, seam sides down.

Bake for 15-20 minutes, or until golden brown. Serve warm or at room temperature.

# Falafel

Biting into a crisp, freshly made falafel can be a truly joyful experience. Make a batch of these once and you'll never be able to eat the mealy, dry, shop-bought version again. They are incredibly easy to make and, after soaking the chickpeas overnight, the preparation time is so minimal that you can have them on your table in 20 minutes.

One rule I must insist on, though: falafel must be eaten as soon as they are made, so have your accompaniments ready before you start frying. Set the table with flatbreads, sliced tomatoes and cucumbers, tahini sauce or hummus, pickles and the hot pepper sauce of your choice. Falafel benefit from these, as they add brightness, texture and heat to each bite.

**Makes 20**

1 1/4 cups/250g dried chickpeas
1 teaspoon cumin seeds
1 teaspoon coriander seeds
1/4 teaspoon ground turmeric
sea salt and freshly ground black pepper
2 scallions, finely sliced
2 garlic cloves, crushed
small handful of cilantro, leaves and slim stems
2 tablespoons all-purpose flour
1/2 teaspoon baking powder
sunflower or vegetable oil, to deep-fry

Soak the chickpeas in a bowl of cold water for at least 8 hours, or overnight.

The next day, prepare your spices by toasting the cumin and coriander seeds in a dry pan over a medium heat for a minute or so until their aromas are released. Grind the seeds in a mortar and pestle.

Drain the chickpeas and place them in a food processor with the spices, seasoning with 1 1/2 teaspoons salt and 1/2 teaspoon pepper, and blitz until smooth. Add the scallions and garlic and pulse again. Finally, add the cilantro, flour and baking powder and blend again until the herbs are well chopped and evenly dispersed.

Roll the chickpea mixture into 20 small balls, each about 2 in./5cm wide, then flatten them slightly between your palms.

Fill a deep pan with oil to 2 in./5cm deep and place over a medium-high heat. The oil needs to be very hot and you can test to see this by dropping a crumb of falafel mixture into the pan: if it sizzles, it is ready.

Carefully drop a few of the falafel into the pan and fry them for a few minutes, turning once, until golden brown all over. Try not to overcrowd the pan, as that will reduce the temperature of the oil; it is better to fry them in batches. Drain the falafel on paper towels and serve immediately.

# Quick pickled avocados

For someone as impatient as me, this was a wonderful discovery, as it magically transforms firm, unripe avocados into delectably soft and tangy morsels after just a few hours. No longer do you have to wait for avos to soften in your fruit bowl, just douse them in this sour and salty brine for a few hours and they will be ready to enjoy alongside rice pilafs or *mazzeh* (mezze) dishes. These are best eaten on the day you make them. Avoid the coriander seeds and peppercorns, as they can be intense when eaten whole.

**Serves 4–6 as part of a spread**

1 cup/250ml white wine vinegar
3 garlic cloves
1 tablespoon sugar
1 tablespoon sea salt
1 teaspoon black peppercorns
1 teaspoon coriander seeds
2 unripe avocados

Place all the ingredients, apart from the avocados, in a saucepan over a medium heat and pour in 1 cup/250ml water. Bring to the boil, stirring every now and then to dissolve the sugar and salt. Let the brine cool to room temperature.

When the brine is cold, peel the avocados, halve them and remove the pits, then cut them into ¼ in./1cm-thick slices. Place them in a 1-quart/1-liter pickling jar or medium plastic container and pour over the brine, making sure you completely cover the avocados. Refrigerate for 2 hours, or up to 6 hours, before serving.

# 3 fermented pickles

Before pickling, be sure to sterilize the jar or jars by washing thoroughly and then placing in an oven preheated to 300°F/150°C for about 10 minutes. Remove and leave to cool.

Take your time to remove any air bubbles from your jar once filled, as these can cause the pickles to go moldy. You can do this in a few different ways. I firmly tap the jar on a work top to release bubbles, then examine the sides of the jar for remaining air pockets and use a knife to poke every one out.

Keep the vegetables fully submerged under the brine. You can do this by wedging a cabbage or cauliflower leaf into the top of the jar to push the vegetables down into the liquid, thus sealing them from any oxygen. If the seal starts to go moldy after a few days, replace it with a fresh leaf.

Place the pickles in a relatively warm place (140°–160°F/60–70°C) for 1 week. Every day, 'burp' the jar by opening it to release any pressure that has built up.

After a few days, you will begin to see bubbles forming in the brine: this is a sign that the pickles are fermenting! The bubbles will calm down after 6–7 days, which shows the pickles are ready to eat. The longer you leave them, the more pronounced the flavor and the higher the levels of good bacteria. Refrigerate after opening and eat within 1 week.

## Pickled turnips with beet

When fermented, turnips take on a radish-like flavor with a wondrous tang and make for a crunchy and delicious snack at any time, or addition to a spread. I always add these to hummus and falafel wraps.

**Makes enough to fill a 3-quart/3-liter jar**

5 turnips
1 beet
2 tablespoons sea salt

3 garlic cloves
cabbage or cauliflower leaf, to seal the jar

Peel the turnips and beet and slice into sticks ¼ in./1cm thick.

Place 3 cups/750ml water and the salt in a large saucepan over a medium heat and bring to the boil, stirring to ensure the salt dissolves. Once the water has boiled, take it off the heat.

Place the garlic cloves in a sterilized 3-quart/3-liter pickling jar (see above) with the turnips and beet, leaving about 2 in./5cm free at the top of the jar. Pour the hot brine over the vegetables, again leaving about 2 in./5cm at the top of the jar.

Remove air bubbles, wedge in a cabbage or cauliflower leaf, then seal and ferment (see above for detailed instructions).

# Pickled cucumbers

Cucumbers for pickling have to be fresh so they stay nice and crunchy, so buy and use the firmest you can find. As the very small mini-cucumbers used in Palestinian food can be difficult to find in the West, I sometimes have to use small regular English cucumbers for these and slice them into thick wedges.

**Makes enough to fill a 3-quart/3-liter jar**

5 Persian cucumbers (or see recipe introduction)
2 tablespoons sea salt
3 garlic cloves
1 sprig of dill

2 red bird's eye chillies, left whole
cabbage or cauliflower leaf, to seal the jar

Slice each cucumber into 4 wedges, or cut them into rounds about ¾ in./2cm thick on the diagonal.

Pour 2¾ cups/650ml water into a large saucepan, add the salt, place over a medium heat and bring to the boil, stirring to ensure the salt dissolves. Remove from the heat.

Place the garlic cloves, dill, whole chillies and cucumbers in a sterilized 3-quart/3-liter pickling jar (see page 64). Pour the hot brine over, leaving about 2 in./5cm at the top of the jar.

Remove air bubbles, wedge in a cabbage or cauliflower leaf, seal and ferment (see page 64 for detailed instructions).

# Pickled cauliflower and carrots

These crunchy, spicy pickles take on a vibrant yellow hue as a result of the turmeric in the pickling brine, and have a special affinity with grilled meat and rice dishes.

**Makes enough to fill a 3-quart/3-liter jar**

1¼ lb./600g cauliflower (about 1 medium-large)
2 large carrots
2 garlic cloves
2 tablespoons sea salt
½ teaspoon ground turmeric
1 teaspoon curry powder
1 red bird's eye chilli, left whole
cabbage or cauliflower leaf, to seal the jar

Cut the cauliflower into small florets about 1 in./3cm thick. Peel the carrots and slice them into diagonal chunks about ¼ in./1cm thick. Halve the garlic cloves.

Place 2¾ cups/650ml water and the salt in a large saucepan over a medium heat. Bring to the boil. Simmer for 1 minute, stirring to dissolve the salt, then turn off the heat, add the ground spices and stir well.

Place the garlic cloves in a sterilized 3-quart/3-liter pickling jar (see page 64) along with the vegetables and whole chilli, leaving about 2 in./5cm at the top of the jar. Pour the hot spiced brine over the vegetables, again leaving about 2 in./5cm at the top of the jar

Remove air bubbles, wedge in a cabbage or cauliflower leaf, then seal and ferment (see page 64 for detailed instructions).

# Haifa and Akka

The coastal city of Haifa in the north-west of Israel is a modern port town, built on the gentle slopes of the Carmel Mountains. Haifa is a sprawling city, a haphazard mix of industrial buildings and modern apartment blocks set against the dazzling backdrop of the Mediterranean Sea. The city's cuisine reflects its modernity, with a vast array of excellent high-end and casual eateries, which incorporate a multitude of influences in the dishes they serve.

I was staying in the Hader neighborhood, just a short stroll away from the emerald lawns and colorful flowerbeds of the Baha'i gardens, Haifa's crowning attraction, where thousands of Baha'i pilgrims flock each year to visit the tomb of their prophet, Baha'u'llah.

I started my day with breakfast at a Palestinian café at the end of the street, where I was invited to share a meal with graphic designer Haitham Haddad. Against a soundtrack of Fairuz, the iconic Lebanese singer whose voice you regularly hear in Palestinian homes and cafés in the early mornings, he ordered us za'atar focaccia with a side of creamy labneh, and a crisp fattoush salad made with peppery arugula and topped with mounds of grated *akkawi* cheese, a local speciality which resembles a kind of salted mozzarella.

Haitham studied graphic design and now owns an avant-garde design studio in the city. He's also an avid baker. "My soul food is bread," he told me in his thick, laid-back drawl as he helped himself to triangles of olive oil-drenched, dimpled focaccia. "I bake a lot and love experimenting with flavors in my loaves, such as sumac or cumin. My body is probably 50 percent dough."

Bread has a special place in Palestinian cuisine: not only does it form an essential component of meals, but the act of breaking bread with another person symbolizes connection and friendship. "The bread and salt between us" is a popular phrase in Arabic, referring to a bond built on respect and comradeship through eating together.

"I can survive on bread, tomato and labneh alone," Haitham told me, not the first time I've heard such assertions from Palestinians. "Our best food is our simplest," he continued. "One of my favorite food memories is of gathering with my family for the olive harvest. My grandmother would come to the fields carrying platters of deep-fried eggplant and cauliflower, with some labneh and bread. We ate it under the trees and it was so simple, so delicious."

He glanced down at the fattoush, keen to make another point, "But to really get the flavor of the home kitchen you have to cut vegetables a certain way." He gestured to the equal-sized squares of tomatoes in the salad. "That's restaurant cooking, but when I think of tomatoes cut into thick triangles, that's my grandmother's Palestinian home cooking."

—

Like many other Middle Eastern cultures, Palestinians value home cooking above

restaurant meals and so it is no surprise that some of the best restaurants embody the spirit of family cooking. The next evening, I visited Douzan, a Palestinian restaurant run by its exuberant owner, Fadi Najir, whose mother and aunts cook in the kitchen. The interior feels like a family home, filled with antique furniture, bookcases and vintage handicrafts that span eighty years. The lack of uniformity is deliberate, Fadi told me. "I choose diversity among the tables to reflect the diversity among humans." Fadi embraces that diversity, circling the restaurant, welcoming diners of all faiths and backgrounds with warmth and hospitality.

Douzan is famed for its *mazzeh* (mezze), so I began feasting on small plates inspired by food from The Galilee. I started with crunchy fried *kibbeh*, small rugby ball-shaped domes of ground lamb encased in bulgur shells and eaten alongside a finely chopped tabbouleh salad packed with the green goodness of parsley and mint, before moving on to thin cigarillos of stuffed vine leaves, mini discs of pastries topped with lamb and tomatoes, juicy spiced lamb kebabs threaded onto cinnamon sticks, spinach-and-sumac-stuffed *fatayer* parcels and thin strips of fried

eggplant rolled around dense balls of smooth white cheese and herbs. The dishes kept coming. I protested, "Honestly, this is too much, I can't eat any more!" and Fadi laughed. "But this is the Palestinian way," he said. "My mother is in the kitchen and, for her, making food for others is an act of love. We always make more than we need, in case someone else turns up and wants to eat. It is the same for coffee, even if there are just two people, we always make enough for four, just in case someone walks past and wants some."

I asked Fadi why he chose this vintage theme for the restaurant. For a moment, his sparkling eyes dimmed a little. "As long as I can keep celebrating our culture, I can hang on to some of my freedom," he told me solemnly. "During the Nakba (the conflict in 1948–9 that led to the State of Israel being created), we lost our land and our homes, many people were expelled and of course now there is the Occupation. But just like the olive trees, our roots are deep and connected to this land. No matter what changes above, we are rooted here and nothing can change that." He paused, noticing that I hadn't touched my plate for a while, before breaking into a broad smile. "Now, you must have some dessert!"

The seaside town of Akka (also known as Acre) is just 15 miles from Haifa, yet the differences between the two places could not be more striking. As you walk around the Byzantine cobbled streets, surrounded by an ancient fort, crumbling stone walls and Crusader-era buildings, you're transported to another time. Akka is one of the oldest cities in the world, a place believed to have been continuously inhabited for 4,000 years. In the 1947 United Nations Partition Plan for Palestine, Akka was designated to be part of a future Palestinian state, but while that never materialized, the Palestinian culture of the city remains strong and thousands of tourists flock to this UNESCO World Heritage site each year.

I arrived in the early morning and began my day walking through the town's old city market just as vendors were setting up their stalls. Fresh fruit and vegetable stands jostled for space with clothing and household goods, as well as handicrafts aimed at the city's many tourists. I was on a mission to find fresh fish and asked the market seller to gut, fillet and fry it for me at the market in anticipation of making *sayadieh*, a regional speciality of spiced rice topped with fried onions and fried fish.

As the sun rose, so did the heat of the day, so I bought a glass of fresh pomegranate juice and walked up to drink it on the outer edges of the fort, sitting on the rocks that look out to sea. The atmosphere was that of a holiday seaside town and the air carried the salty scent of the ocean. Fishermen were sitting silently on the rocks, patiently waiting for their daily catches. Children carried balloons on the backs of ponies, enjoying short rides along the seafront, while playful teenage boys stripped off their shirts, raced along the walls and jumped 300 feet down into the sea, cheering each other on with their bravado.

I finished my juice and headed off to meet Hajji Monira, a sprightly woman in her seventies who is an active member of the community, working for local charities and women's associations. She is also a gifted cook and we spent the day dissecting the traditions of Palestinian cooking.

As we busied ourselves, I glanced around at the framed black-and-white pictures that decorate her home, pictures that tell the story of her life. Hajji Monira was born in Akka but fled to Lebanon as a refugee during the 1948–9 Nakba. She was one of the lucky few from her community who were able to return, and has spent her life engaged in community and charitable activities to keep Palestinian culture alive in the city.

She also caters for events and is a stern cooking teacher, so every time my questions wandered off to her memories of Lebanon, or what happened to the home her family lived in, she firmly guided me back to the task at hand. 'Look! You have to see what color the onions turn, so you know they are ready!' I peered into the pan, noted the golden hue of the translucent onions and promised her I was paying attention.

We saved our history conversations for when we were eating the succulent fish, with its tangle of caramelized onions and fragrant rice.

—

Eating fish is a quintessential part of Akkawi life, a point drummed home the next day when I spent an afternoon cooking with Safa Tamish, the director of the Arab Forum for Sexuality, Education and Health. "Eating fish needs passion!" she told me, animatedly bringing her fingertips together as if to prove her point. "You have to tear it apart with your fingers to really be able to enjoy it. We always used to joke that you can tell when people from the villages come to Akka, because they eat fish with a knife and fork. But the original Akkawi people know that you eat fish with your hands!" I agreed vehemently; whenever I really enjoy a dish, I want to pick at it with my fingers. There's something intimate about eating with one's hands and it undoubtedly elevates the sensory experience of food. Safa nodded in agreement. "Eating with your hands means that you feel what you are eating," she said. "We are born with fingers, not with knives and spoons, so it is much more natural. In the old ages, people used to put food in one large shared plate and I remember, as a child, sitting on the floor eating with my family. It was cosy and brought us together. This cultural aspect of sharing our food is very important."

But Safa wasn't teaching me how to cook fish that day, instead we were immersing ourselves in another delicacy, *sheikh el mahshi*, a dish of mini zucchini stuffed with ground lamb and pine nuts, then cooked in a piquant yogurt sauce. As we began to fry the lamb for the stuffing, Safa's husband Omar leaned over and sniffed. "It needs more spice," he said. "Add a little bit more cinnamon." Gifted with a highly sensitive palate, Omar insists his powerful sense of smell means he can tell what seasoning a dish needs simply by sniffing it. "How wonderful," I exclaimed. "What an incredible gift!" Omar chuckled. "Not really," he said, shaking his head in disagreement. "Traveling is a nightmare. Think about it Yasmin, most smells in the world are not good!"

The lively atmosphere continued when we were joined by Omar's mum, who wanted to teach me how to pound and shape seasoned lamb into *kibbeh*, the prized Levantine bulgur wheat meatball. *Kibbeh* is one of the most iconic recipes of the Levant, in part because it is so labor intensive. Women often make it in groups, sitting together for several hours to pound and mold *kibbeh*.

My skills were somewhat lacking and the others spent about 30 minutes laughing at me, until I finally produced something passable. I was told an old wives' tale that when, in years gone by, men were looking for wives, they would look at a potential bride's hands: do they look like *kibbeh*-making palms? If so, she would make a good wife.

I looked at my lumpy balls of *kibbeh*, somewhat disheartened. "This is probably why I'm single, isn't it?" I sighed, as our laughter punctuated the air.

Omar's mother is originally from Jerusalem but had to flee to Syria during the 1948-9 Nakba and hasn't been able to live in her home city since. She told me that, when they became refugees, they had to stop making *kibbeh* with meat and her grandmother made it with grain or chickpeas instead, a sorry state of affairs. "You'd need a lot of cumin and black pepper to make it taste good," she confided, sorrowfully.

With the women in charge of the meat dishes, Omar started on salad, a personal invention he calls "*adassarian*," a colorful medley of lentils (*adas* in Arabic) tossed with tomatoes and peppers and dressed with a subtle garlic vinaigrette, basil and parsley. An engineer by training, for 13 years Omar also led a dance troupe, Al Fanoon, who performed a joyful Palestinian line dance—*dabkeh*—for feasts and weddings. Omar broke taboos by putting women at the head of his troupe. "It led to so much debate about whether it was authentic," he told me. "And we have the same debate about Palestinian food today, what is authentic and what is modern, what is borrowed, what is imported. How does it relate to Palestinian identity."

I told Omar I had been pondering similar questions on my journey and Omar told me that for him it was simple. "My Palestinian identity is not something I dig up from under the ground. It is something I'm living and creating every day. It's my experience of it that counts, like this dish I invented!"

He gestured to the chopping board where he was slicing peppers and asked me to grate lemon zest and chop basil. "You have to smell the herbs to appreciate them," he told me, and I closed my eyes and inhaled deeply. But even herbs aren't without problems here, Omar told me. "Some are grown in illegal Israeli settlements in the West Bank, then sold to fancy supermarkets in the UK," he said. "As Palestinians, we urge people not to buy these; we feel it gives the settlements a sense of viability and permanence."

In a place where connection to the land is so important yet so strained, it doesn't surprise me that even ingredients for a simple salad are controversial. But as we ate lunch—a feast of two kinds of *kibbeh*, stuffed zucchini, rice speckled with toasted vermicelli, warm *taboon* breads and the flavorsome lentil salad—I was reminded of the Palestinian emphasis on collectivity through food, of making dishes together, of sharing from one plate and "the bread and salt between us" that actively encourages closer connection with others. In a land of division, Palestinians use food to celebrate commonality, an attitude needed here more than anywhere else.

# SALADS

Tangy, crunchy salads or sliced fresh vegetables accompany all Palestinian meals and bring a welcome brightness and freshness to the table, especially during the hot summer months.

Scattered with bold handfuls of fresh herbs, Palestinian salads offer sharp, citrusy flavors as a foil to the warming, soothing spices of a main course. Dressings are kept simple, normally just the winning combination of peppery local olive oil and tangy lemon juice, or perhaps some nutty tahini.

# Roast Romanesco cauliflower with tahini and pomegranates

This is a colorfully cheery dish that is sure to win over even the most ardent cauliflower sceptic. I mean, honestly, who doesn't love food in fractals? (Though you can use regular cauliflower, too.) By roasting the florets, they stay juicy with just the right amount of crunch, ready to be smothered in the ubiquitous Palestinian garlicky tahini sauce. Quick, easy to make and very good for you, this is Palestinian home cooking at its best.

**Serves 4–6 as part of a spread**

### FOR THE CAULIFLOWER
2 heads of Romanesco cauliflower, cut into 2 in./5cm florets
4 tablespoons olive oil or any neutral oil
1 teaspoon ground cumin
1 teaspoon ground allspice
sea salt and freshly ground black pepper
2 tablespoons pomegranate seeds

### FOR THE TAHINI SAUCE
5 teaspoons/75g tahini
4 tablespoons lemon juice
1 garlic clove, crushed

Preheat the oven to 400°F/200°C.

Place the cauliflower florets on a large baking sheet and drizzle over the cooking oil, cumin and allspice. Season generously with salt and pepper and give the florets a good stir so they are evenly coated.

Transfer to the oven and cook for 20–30 minutes, until the cauliflower is tender but still firm, tossing halfway through to make sure the florets cook evenly. Leave them to cool slightly while you make the sauce.

Whisk together all the ingredients for the tahini sauce with 7 tablespoons/100ml water and season with salt and pepper.

Once the cauliflower has reached room temperature, place on a platter, drizzle over the tahini sauce and sprinkle with the pomegranate seeds.

# Everyday Palestinian salad

If you are going to serve just one vegetable dish alongside a Palestinian meal, then make it this classic Middle Eastern combination of crunchy vegetables dressed with lemon juice and olive oil. Be sure to cut all the vegetables into equal-sized pieces, so each mouthful delivers all the ingredients together.

**Serves 4 as a side dish**

4 Persian cucumbers, or 10 oz./350g (about 1) regular English cucumber
3 medium tomatoes
1 red pepper
3 tablespoons/10g parsley leaves, finely chopped
3 tablespoons/10g mint leaves, finely chopped
3 tablespoons extra virgin olive oil
juice of 1 lemon, or to taste
sea salt and freshly ground black pepper

Slice the cucumbers in half and use a teaspoon to scoop out and discard their watery seeds. Finely chop, so each piece is about 1/4 in./1cm.

Scoop the seeds out of the tomatoes and slice into pieces the same size as the cucumber. Do the same with the red pepper and place all the vegetables in a large bowl.

Dress the salad with the herbs, extra virgin olive oil, lemon juice and a good sprinkling of salt and pepper. Taste and adjust the seasoning to your taste; it is supposed to be sharp, so add extra lemon juice if necessary.

# Roast rainbow carrots with herbed yogurt

This recipe is inspired by a meal I enjoyed at Tawla, a Palestinian-owned restaurant in San Francisco that serves up innovative and tasty adaptations of Eastern Mediterranean cuisine. Rainbow carrots are a particular addiction of mine and I adore how they brighten up my table with their purple and golden hues. If you can't find any, fear not, regular carrots will do, just try and buy organic if you can as the taste is so much better. This salad is best made an hour or so in advance, then left to rest so the carrots soak up all the herby flavors from the dressing.

**Serves 4 as part of a spread**

2 lb./1kg mixed rainbow carrots (ideally purple, white and orange)
3 tablespoons extra virgin olive oil
sea salt and freshly ground black pepper
3 tablespoons unflavored yogurt

1 garlic clove, crushed
1 teaspoon finely chopped fresh dill, or 1/2 teaspoon dried dill
1 teaspoon dried mint
1/2 teaspoon nigella seeds
3/4 teaspoon sesame seeds

Preheat the oven to 400°F/200°C.

Peel the carrots and slice them diagonally into thick wedges. Toss them with 2 tablespoons of the extra virgin olive oil and 1/4 teaspoon salt and roast for 30–35 minutes, until they are tender, but still have some bite.

Meanwhile, whisk together all the remaining ingredients, except the seeds, (and not forgetting the final 1 tablespoon extra virgin olive oil) with 1/4 teaspoon each salt and pepper.

When the carrots are ready, transfer them to a serving dish and leave them to cool to room temperature. Pour over the yogurt dressing, mix well, then taste and adjust the seasoning. Scatter with the nigella and sesame seeds.

You can tuck in immediately or, for best results, cover and leave to rest for about 1 hour before serving.

Pictured on previous page

# Gazan salad

This salad epitomizes Gazan cuisine for me, with its holy trinity of dill, green chilli and garlic. It's a punchy little number that is best served alongside milder dishes. Try it with Roast chicken stuffed with raisins and pine nuts or *Maqloubeh* (see pages 174 and 142). As the size and heat of chillies will vary, be sure to adjust the spiciness of this as you prefer.

**Serves 4 as a side dish**

3 Persian cucumbers, or 8½ oz./300g (about 1) regular English cucumber
4 medium tomatoes
1 avocado
3 tablespoons finely chopped dill
1–2 green chillies, finely chopped

1 garlic clove, crushed
juice of 1 lemon
4 tablespoons extra virgin olive oil
sea salt and freshly ground black pepper

Cut the cucumbers in half and use a teaspoon to scoop out and discard their watery seeds. Chop the cucumbers into small pieces and place in a bowl.

Halve the tomatoes, then scoop out the seeds and discard them, too. Halve, pit and peel the avocado. Chop the tomatoes and avocado into pieces the same size as the cucumbers and add to the bowl.

Add the dill, 1 chilli, the garlic, lemon juice, extra virgin olive oil, 1/2 teaspoon salt and 1/4 teaspoon pepper and stir well. Taste, adjust the seasoning if needed, add more chilli if you want and serve immediately.

# Fattoush

Infinitely adaptable and wonderfully refreshing, the recipe for this citrusy salad is inspired by a visit to the home of the Palestinian singer Reem Talhami (see page 105), who welcomed me into her kitchen on a hot summer's day in Jerusalem to guide me through the essential components of this Palestinian classic. It is supposed to be quite astringent so, if you enjoy sharper flavors, edge towards including more lemon juice or sumac, adding them in stages, then tasting and adjusting as you like. Go carefully and remember: you can always add more to a recipe, but you can never take away.

**Serves 4 as a side dish**

FOR THE SALAD
2 Middle Eastern flatbreads, or pita breads (around 4 oz./120g in total)
4 tablespoons extra virgin olive oil
3 small Persian cucumbers, or 10 oz./275g (about 1 smallish) regular English cucumber
4 tomatoes (around 14 oz./450g in total)
2½ oz./75g Romaine lettuce, roughly chopped
3 scallions, finely chopped
3 tablespoons/10g mint leaves, finely chopped

6 tablespoons/20g parsley leaves, finely chopped
2½ oz./75g feta cheese, crumbled (optional)

FOR THE DRESSING
1 tablespoon sumac, or to taste
3 tablespoons lemon juice, or to taste
4 tablespoons extra virgin olive oil, plus more if needed
sea salt and freshly ground black pepper

Preheat the oven to 400°F/200°C. Toss the breads with the extra virgin olive oil, then bake them in the oven for about 10 minutes, or until very crisp. Allow to cool, then break into thick shards.

Cut the cucumbers in half and use a teaspoon to remove and discard the watery seeds. Chop into ¼–½ in./1–2cm pieces and place in a serving bowl.

Cut the tomatoes in half, scoop out their seeds, cut them into pieces the same size as the cucumber and add to the bowl with the bread shards. Add the remaining vegetables and the herbs.

Mix all the ingredients for the salad dressing, add it to the bowl and use your hands to mix it all together. I was instructed by Reem that this was the most important part and it gives you a feel for the dish, letting you know, for instance, if you need to add more oil. Taste and adjust the seasoning to your preference and, if you are adding feta, crumble it over just before serving.

# Tabbouleh

On my first trip to the West Bank, I heard an old saying: a woman who can make a good tabbouleh makes a good wife. Presumably that is because you need the patience of a saint to chop the herbs into the finest of pieces. This is one of those dishes that does require chopping the herbs by hand, as blitzing them in a food processor can leave them mushy, so take your time and enjoy it as a meditative process. It is well worth the effort, and this aromatic salad is the perfect complement to the richer stews and grilled meats of Palestinian cuisine. Traditionally, fine bulgur wheat is used. I prefer the texture of a thicker grain, but just use whichever you have to hand.

**Serves 4 as a side dish**

⅓ cup/40g bulgur wheat
3 tomatoes
2 scallions
5 oz./150g parsley leaves
1 oz./30g mint leaves

juice of 2 lemons
4 tablespoons extra virgin olive oil
sea salt and freshly ground black pepper

Cook the bulgur wheat in a pan of boiling water according to the packet instructions. Drain, rinse with cold water and set aside in a sieve or fine colander to drain very well.

Slice the tomatoes in half and scoop out the seeds. Finely chop them into very small pieces. Finely chop the scallions into pieces of the same size. Finely chop the herbs, getting them as small as you can, and place them in a bowl with the tomatoes and scallions. Add the bulgur.

Dress the salad with the lemon juice, extra virgin olive oil, ¾ teaspoon salt and ¼ teaspoon pepper. Stir well to ensure that everything is well combined, then taste and adjust the seasoning. Serve. The dressing will make the herb leaves turn soggy quite quickly, but it is not the end of the world if you leave it for 1 hour; in fact, I often finish it off for lunch the next day if I've got leftovers and it still tastes great.

# Donyana salad

This aromatic recipe draws inspiration from a dish I enjoyed on the breezy seafront terrace of Donyana restaurant in the historic coastal town of Akka. The city is a UNESCO World Heritage site and has a long history; it is mentioned in Egyptian texts from the nineteenth century BC, while in Greek mythology it is supposedly the place where Hercules found a medicinal plant to heal his wounds. Donyana is a derivative of the word that means 'the world' in Arabic and, wandering through the city's ancient winding streets and Ottoman-era fort, the mélange of influences that have gathered here over the centuries is tangible. Paying homage to that, this glorious mixture of textures and flavors celebrates local Palestinian ingredients.

**Serves 4 as a side dish**

2 fennel bulbs (about 8 oz./300g in total)
1 Granny Smith apple, or other tart apple
3 tablespoons/15g dill, coarse stalks removed, finely chopped
3 tablespoons/15g parsley leaves, finely chopped
¼ cup/30g sweetened dried cranberries or sour cherries
⅓ cup/50g blanched almonds, roughly chopped

juice of ½ orange, or to taste
juice of ½ lemon, or to taste
zest of 1 organic or unwaxed orange, removed with a zester
2 tablespoons extra virgin olive oil
sea salt and freshly ground black pepper

Core the fennel and apple and, using a sharp knife or mandoline, finely cut both into very thin slices, saving any fennel fronds. Place in a bowl with the herbs and cranberries or cherries.

Toast the almonds in a dry pan over a medium heat until they turn golden brown, then add them to the salad.

Pour over the orange and lemon juices, orange zest and extra virgin olive oil and season with salt and pepper. Toss gently and taste; you may want to add a squeeze more lemon or orange juice to adjust the acidity or sweetness to your liking. Scatter with the reserved fennel fronds, if you have them.

This salad can happily sit for 1 hour or so before serving; in fact it even improves, as the flavors have a chance to harmonize.

# Eggplant, tomato and pomegranate salad

SALATIT EL BATINJAN

Eggplants and pomegranates are a classic Middle Eastern food pairing that never fails to satisfy and delight. This is a dish of Lebanese origin which is now enjoyed throughout The Galilee; the addition of warming allspice gives a distinctly Palestinian flavor.

**Serves 4-6 as part of a spread**

FOR THE DRESSING

2 tablespoons unsweetened pomegranate molasses
3 tablespoons extra virgin olive oil
2 garlic cloves, crushed
1 tablespoon lemon juice
1/4 teaspoon ground allspice
sea salt and freshly ground black pepper

FOR THE SALAD

3 large eggplants
extra virgin olive oil
4 medium tomatoes (around 1 lb./500g in total), seeds removed, chopped
2 scallions, finely sliced
seeds of 1/2 pomegranate, plus more to serve
1/2 oz./15g parsley leaves, finely chopped, plus more to serve
1/2 oz./15g mint leaves, finely chopped, plus more to serve

Place all the dressing ingredients in a clean jam jar, seasoning with 3/4 teaspoon salt and 1/4 teaspoon pepper. Screw on the lid and give it a good shake so that the ingredients combine. Set the dressing aside for the flavors to infuse while you make the salad.

Preheat the oven to 350°F/180°C.

Peel the eggplants if you like, chop them into 1 in./3cm chunks and place them on a baking sheet. Drizzle over a couple of tablespoons extra virgin olive oil and 1/2 teaspoon salt and use your hands to mix it all together. Roast for about 25 minutes, or until they are soft.

Transfer the eggplant to a serving bowl and leave to cool.

Add the remaining salad ingredients to the bowl and pour over the dressing. Mix well, then taste to adjust the seasoning.

Sprinkle with a few more pomegranate seeds and herbs just before serving.

# Radicchio, radish and clementine salad

This sweet and bitter winter salad was inspired by a meal I shared in the home of a food grower and community campaigner living in Ramallah, who goes by the name of Sumood wa Hurriya (literally 'steadfastness and freedom'). Sumood is passionate about promoting local and seasonal Palestinian foods and the salad was her way of showing off her favorite local winter ingredients. Removing the segments from the clementines isn't strictly necessary here, but it will make a difference to the taste and texture of the dish. If you don't feel the urge to do it, simply make sure to meticulously remove all the pith from each slice of fruit.

**Serves 4 as a side dish**

### FOR THE DRESSING
1 garlic clove
1¼ tablespoons apple cider vinegar
2 tablespoons extra virgin olive oil
½ tablespoon date syrup (optional)
finely grated zest of 1 unwaxed or organic clementine
sea salt and freshly ground black pepper

### FOR THE SALAD
3 clementines, or other small winter citrus fruits
3 oz./100g arugula
2¼ oz./65g radicchio, roughly chopped
2 oz./50g radishes, quartered
2 oz./50g Medjool dates, pitted and roughly chopped
2 tablespoons pumpkin or sunflower seeds

Using the flat side of the blade of a large knife, smash the garlic clove, then place it in an empty jar and add the rest of the dressing ingredients, seasoning with ¼ teaspoon each salt and pepper. Screw the lid on the jar and shake vigorously. Leave to infuse while you assemble the salad.

Remove the segments from the clementines: slice the top and bottom off the first one, cutting deep enough that you see a wheel of clementine flesh on both sides. Place the fruit on one of its flat ends, then slice off the remaining peel and pith, following the contour of the fruit. To remove individual segments, insert your knife as close as you can to the inside membrane of each segment and cut to the core. Do the same for both sides of the segment; it should release with no pith. Repeat with the remaining clementines.

Place the segments in a bowl with the arugula, radicchio, radishes and dates.

Toast the seeds by stirring them in a dry pan over a medium heat for a minute or so, until golden. Tip them into the salad.

Remove the garlic from the dressing and pour over the salad, mixing to coat the leaves. Serve immediately.

# Freekeh with butternut squash and kale

This dish is inspired by the first meal my photographer Raya cooked for me after my exhausting airport ordeal (see page 8). It is a hearty and healthy vegetarian pilaf which uplifts and soothes in equal measure, and it is a great introduction to freekeh, the smoky and nutty Palestinian grain. Serve with a dollop of Greek yogurt and a fresh green salad.

**Serves 4**

1⅓ lb./600g butternut squash, peeled and deseeded, sliced into ¾ in./2cm-thick wedges
olive oil or any neutral oil
1 tablespoon honey, or maple syrup
¾ teaspoon ground allspice
sea salt and freshly ground black pepper
1 cup/150g freekeh
10 oz./350g kale, coarse stalks removed, chopped
1 onion, finely chopped

3 garlic cloves, crushed
14 oz./400g can of chickpeas, drained and rinsed
juice and finely grated zest of ½ unwaxed lemon
generous pinch of freshly ground nutmeg
1 cup/100g walnut pieces
seeds from ½ pomegranate
2 scallions, finely chopped
Greek yogurt, to serve

Preheat the oven to 400°F/200°C. Place the squash on a baking sheet and pour over 2 tablespoons cooking oil, the honey (or syrup), ¼ teaspoon allspice, ¼ teaspoon salt and a generous grind of pepper. Use your hands to mix it all together, then bake for 20-25 minutes, until the squash is soft.

Cook the freekeh in a pan of boiling water with ½ teaspoon salt for 25 minutes. For the last few minutes, add the kale, cover and cook until it is cooked to your liking (depending on the season and variety of kale, 2-6 minutes). Rinse in cold water and drain.

Heat 2 tablespoons cooking oil in a large saucepan and fry the onion over a low heat for 15 minutes, until soft. Add the garlic, reduce the heat and fry for a few minutes. Add the chickpeas, lemon juice and zest, nutmeg, kale and freekeh and remaining ½ teaspoon allspice. Season with ½ teaspoon each salt and pepper and stir well. Taste and adjust the seasoning, turn into a serving dish and add the squash.

Toast the walnuts in a dry pan over a medium heat for a few minutes until they turn glossy. Scatter them over the pilaf with the pomegranate seeds and scallions, then serve with thick dollops of creamy Greek yogurt on the side.

# Red pepper, lentil and tomato salad

"ADASSARIAN"

This wonderfully fragrant salad works well both as a *mazzeh* (mezze) and as a more substantial main course. I learned to make it at the home of Omar Barghouti, who wanted to show me this recipe in part to showcase his love of lentils. *Adas* means "lentils" in Arabic and the name of the dish came about after Omar was teased by a friend one day for never eating lamb and following a vegetarian diet. After serving him this lentil dish, his friend said to him, "But you eat so much *adas*, you can't call yourself vegetarian, you must be an *adassarian!*" Hence the Arabic name above.

**Serves 4–6 as part of a spread, or 2–3 as a main course**

1 cup/200g brown or green lentils
5 tablespoons apple cider vinegar
½ small red onion, finely chopped
juice of ½ lemon, or to taste
5 tablespoons extra virgin olive oil
1 red pepper, chopped into ¼ in./1cm pieces
5 oz./150g red or yellow cherry tomatoes, quartered
finely grated zest of 1 unwaxed lemon
1 garlic clove, crushed
3½ tablespoons/15g basil leaves, roughly torn, plus more to serve
sea salt and freshly ground black pepper
2½ oz./75g feta cheese, crumbled (optional)

Cook the lentils in a saucepan of simmering water until they are soft but still have some bite. Depending on the freshness of the lentils, this will take 15–20 minutes.

Meanwhile, pour the vinegar into a small bowl and add the red onion. Stir well, then leave the onion to soak (this removes some of its pungency).

Once the lentils are cooked, drain them, rinse with warm water and place in a serving bowl. Immediately squeeze over the lemon juice and 2 tablespoons extra virgin olive oil and stir well. Leave to cool completely.

Stir in the red onion (drain and reserve the vinegar for the dressing), red pepper, tomatoes, lemon zest, garlic and basil.

Dress the salad by stirring through 2 tablespoons of the reserved vinegar, the remaining 3 tablespoons extra virgin olive oil, 1 teaspoon salt and ½ teaspoon pepper. Mix well, then taste and adjust the seasoning. You may want to add a bit more of the vinegar, lemon juice or salt to balance out the flavors.

Just before serving, strew with a few more basil leaves and the feta, if you are using it.

# Chickpea and bulgur salad

Nutty and flavorsome, packed with herbs and zingy flavors, this makes a great side dish for roasted meat and fish. Try it with Lemon, cumin and green chilli sea bass, or Slow-roast shoulder of lamb with Palestinian spices (see pages 154 and 189), or it is lovely on its own as a light vegetarian main dish.

**Serves 4–6 as part of a spread, or 2–3 as a main course**

1 1/3 cups/175g coarse bulgur wheat
sea salt and freshly ground black pepper
14 oz./400g can of chickpeas, drained and rinsed
1/2 cup/30g parsley leaves, finely chopped
1/2 cup/30g mint leaves, finely chopped

3 1/2 tablespoons/15g chives, finely chopped
2 garlic cloves, crushed
5 tablespoons extra virgin olive oil
juice of 2 lemons
1/3 cup/60g pomegranate seeds

Cook the bulgur wheat with 1/2 teaspoon salt in a large saucepan of boiling water for 10 minutes, or until it is soft. Drain, rinse with cold water and place in a large serving bowl.

Add the chickpeas to the bulgur wheat, then stir through the chopped herbs and garlic. Dress the salad with the extra virgin olive oil, lemon juice, 1 teaspoon salt and 1/2 teaspoon pepper. Taste and adjust the seasoning as you prefer, bearing in mind that this dish benefits from generous salting.

Just before serving, sprinkle over the pomegranate seeds.

# Jerusalem

On my first morning in Jerusalem, I woke up early and headed straight to the rooftop of my hotel, nestled in the heart of the walled old city. The sun had just begun its slow ascent through the sky and, as I sipped my cardamom-spiked coffee, I gazed out upon the densely concentrated assortment of houses and apartments, interspersed with religious sites and historical buildings. My eyes paused, just for a moment, on the golden sphere of the Dome of the Rock, glistening in the middle distance.

As I waited for my breakfast—the Palestinian staple of hummus, flatbread, sliced tomatoes and olives—I was captivated by the glimpses of ordinary life revealed from where I was sitting. The mothers carrying baskets of wet clothes to their roofs to hang on the washing line; the stray cats running in and out of hidden corners; the clatter of market vendors setting up their stalls; the heady scent of za'atar beginning to rise through the air.

—

The old city of Jerusalem represents the beating heart of the Palestinian community and bursts with life and vibrancy. The city's walls and gates in their current formation were built in the sixteenth century during Ottoman rule, and today it is split into four distinct quarters: Arab, Jewish, Christian and Armenian. The main entrance for the Arab quarter is Damascus Gate and, upon entering, I paused in the doorway under the watchful eyes of the teenage Israeli soldiers who police the area, and bought a large bunch of sage from the Palestinian women who crouch on the floor at makeshift stalls. I wanted it to flavor small cups of black tea, a new, welcome discovery for me—an ardent tea drinker—but common in Palestine.

Entering the cobbled streets of the walled city, I headed straight for the glorious assortment of seasonal fruits on display and grabbed a few favorites—pomegranates, figs and peaches—to snack on later. Tourists were beginning to throng through the small passages of the souk, which sells everything from freshly baked bread and sweet flaky pastries to vegetables, meat and dairy and household goods such as ceramics, clothes and textiles. The old city is the kind of place a hungry traveler can relish getting lost in; simply follow your nose down winding streets to spice sellers, exquisite kebab makers and moreish halva confectioners.

—

After spending the morning walking through the narrow passageways, sampling as many crunchy sesame and fennel *ka'ak* biscuits as is decently permissible, I made my way out of the walled gates and walked deeper into East Jerusalem to meet Essa Grayeb, a Palestinian rheumatology nurse, for lunch. We met in the courtyard of the Zahra Hotel, a dark, crumbling building that has seen better days. But we came for the food not the décor and Essa ordered *kefte bil tahini*,

a sumptuous dish of spiced lamb meatballs baked over thin slices of potatoes, then smothered in a garlicky warm tahini sauce.

"Jerusalem can seem very charming to tourists," Essa said, as he cut through his *kefte* and delicately dipped it in the tahini. "But actually, it's a really tough place to live. It feels like a pressure cooker. It is a divided city and you can't take it out of that context. If you live in Haifa you might not see the Occupation, but here, we exist with it every day."

In the original UN partition plan for Palestine in 1947, Jerusalem was given to international administration, but what followed was a bloody war that led to a divided city, with the Israeli population settling in the West and the Palestinian population in the East. In 1967, the Israeli army captured the Old City and, along with the rest of East Jerusalem, annexed it as Israeli territory. Today the Israeli government continues to control East Jerusalem, which it considers part of its national capital. Palestinians, the United Nations Security Council and the international community at large, however, see East Jerusalem as part of the Occupied Palestinian Territories.

"I think that, just dealing with the cuisine, you will see a romantic view of Jerusalem life," Essa continued. "But that doesn't reflect our reality." Essa wasn't the first Palestinian to challenge me on writing about food culture in a region fraught with conflict. Over the last 70 years, Palestine and its citizens have been over-researched and over-interviewed by journalists, NGO workers, UN officials and elected representatives alike, and there run deep feelings of frustration at so many people documenting their situation while so little changes. One frustrated woman angrily told me: "We are not clowns in a circus for you to come and watch and make research notes about and then make your name from writing down our suffering." It was a comment that touched me deeply.

"I understand that you want to share our culture," Essa continued, politely but pointedly. "But you can't discuss Palestinian food without talking about the Occupation. About the water restrictions, about the inability to move freely, about the checkpoints, about the house demolitions. This isn't me being political, this is me explaining that the Occupation affects how we eat. You can't escape it."

—

It was a conversation I continued the next day with singer Reem Talhami, who echoed Essa's sentiments. "From the very beginning, Jerusalem is heavy," she told me, inhaling deeply on her cigarette. "The moment you get into the city, you feel it in the air."

Tall, striking and beautiful, Reem embodies Palestinian passion and has the remarkable gift of being able to translate it into song. We met at her house to make fattoush, a Palestinian staple and one of my all-time favorite dishes of the region, a sharp and tangy salad of crisp lettuce, juicy tomatoes, crunchy cucumbers, chopped parsley and mint, flecked with toasted shards of bread. Fattoush is exactly the kind of food I want to eat on a hot summer's day, refreshing and uplifting all at once. It is a dish that has the ability to instantly lift the mood, with its enlivening dressing made from extra virgin olive oil, lemon juice and sumac, an astringent, citrusy and vibrant seasoning made from the ground berries of the native sumac bush.

As we chopped and sliced the vegetables, Reem talked about her work as a singer. "I wanted to use my voice to share the story of Palestinians," Reem told me. "To tell our side through the song, to help uplift my people. This has been my mission." She handed me a large bunch of parsley and I began to strip away its coarse stems and transfer the leaves to a chopping board for slicing.

"But it's hard in Jerusalem," she continued, scraping chunks of cucumber off the wooden board and into a large terracotta serving bowl. "It's a city that you love and hate at the same time. I am raising three daughters here and there are lots of challenges for girls in a city that is becoming increasingly religious. My daughters are full of talents—they dance, sing and act—but the lack of freedom of movement with the checkpoints is very hard. If my daughter is accepted into Birzeit University (in the West Bank), then traveling from there to Jerusalem every day is too hard. She will have to endure so many hours on the road and go through all of that humiliation at the checkpoints."

Reem grabbed a tall, dark bottle of extra virgin olive oil from the cupboard and started assembling ingredients for the dressing. "How does it feel for you?" I asked. "Going through these checkpoints?" Reem sighed and paused for a moment, putting the bottle down. "It depends on how the soldier feels. We have lived with the soldiers for many years now, I've been meeting them at checkpoints in my teens, my twenties, my thirties. I met them as a child, a young woman, a wife, a mother. I've grown up with them. Sometimes the soldier is human, sometimes he's a monster, sometimes he's a sort of god dictating your day. Sometimes he's just a little boy who doesn't want to be there, who just wants to be at the beach with his girlfriend, having a swim or sharing a kiss." We went back to our chopping for a while, in silence.

"Sometimes the soldiers cry, sometimes they shoot their guns, sometimes they kill. Psychologically, the unpredictability of the Occupation is what makes you feel so insecure... your day is not in your hands.

"For millions of people around the world, Jerusalem is some mythological, magical place. But for me, it's not that, it's not something that is at all sentimental, it's my daily life. And the people who live here are having a really hard time under all the pressure. That's why they lose hope and do crazy things."

Out of all the places I'd traveled in Israel and the West Bank, Jerusalem undoubtedly felt the most challenging. So it was heartening to spend an evening cooking with Jamal Juma', a community activist who is decidedly upbeat. Jamal is the co-ordinator of Stop the Wall, an umbrella group of organisations who campaign against Israel's Separation Wall, which is being constructed around the West Bank.

The Wall (which has been deemed illegal by the International Court of Justice) cuts through villages and farmland, separating families from each other and communities from essential educational and medical services. Despite the ICJ ruling, the Wall continues to be built and is now more than 60 percent complete. If finished, it is set to measure more than 430 miles/700km, the distance between London and Zurich and four times as long as the Berlin Wall. While the Israeli government claims its purpose is to provide security, the route of the Wall encircles 80 Israeli settlements, suggesting that its primary function is to incorporate these communities into Israel. Jamal, along with many of his colleagues at Stop the Wall, have been arrested, detained and imprisoned without charge by the Israeli authorities for their campaigning.

Despite working on such a challenging issue, Jamal is someone who makes you feel unshakeably positive about the world. A native Jerusalemite, the recipe he showed me how to cook has its roots in the Negev and is a celebratory dish served at feasts or on special occasions. Called *mansaf*, it's a rich and creamy stew of lamb slow-cooked in *jameed* (a type of fermented whey made from ewe's or goat's milk) and served on top of bread and rice. As we stirred the *jameed* into hot water to dissolve it, Jamal cracked jokes about the lack of inspiring leadership within the Palestinian Authority and teased me about the role of the British in creating the situation, when they gave up their mandate in Palestine in 1948.

How can you stay so upbeat, I asked, given the situation you see here every day? Jamal smiled and reached for the lamb pieces that we had trimmed of fat, gently placing chunks of them in the hot broth, one at a time. "It's easy," he said. "I stay hopeful because I believe that apartheid will eventually be defeated. Because history tells us it is not the norm. I don't believe, in the twenty-first century, we need to lock people inside walls in order to get some false sense of security and I know, in my heart, that building walls is not a sign of strength but a sign of weakness."

He dropped the final piece of lamb into the pot, reduced the heat so the stew could cook on a gentle simmer, and firmly placed the lid on. "Remember Yasmin," he said, turning to face me, "walls don't last forever."

# SOUPS

There is a quiet, replenishing nature to soup, a fact that is universally—though silently—acknowledged, as it's a dish we turn to across the globe in times of convalescence or when we're in need of comfort.

Palestinian soups cater for every season and occasion. From herb- and spinach-packed broths the color of a summer lawn, to chunky kale and noodle potages bursting with warmth and vitality. Many of the recipes in this chapter also double up as hearty vegetable stews that are filling enough to be eaten as an entire meal. Palestinians tend to thicken their soups with grains such as rice, *maftool* or freekeh, making them both economical and sustaining, preparing you for anything the world might throw at you.

# Roast pumpkin, sage and maftool soup

Wild sage grows all around Palestinian villages and is a signature flavor added to small cups of black tea. Here it is paired with roasted sweet pumpkin and *maftool*, a type of Palestinian couscous (see page 18), in a comforting bowl of soup.

**Serves 4–6**

2 lb./1kg pumpkin or butternut squash, peeled, deseeded and cut into ¾ in./2cm chunks
4 tablespoons olive oil or any neutral oil
⅓ cup/50g *maftool*
2 tablespoons/30g salted butter
1 onion, finely chopped

2 garlic cloves, crushed
½ teaspoon ground ginger
8 sage leaves, 4 finely chopped, 4 left whole
3 cups/750ml vegetable or chicken stock
sea salt and freshly ground black pepper
extra virgin olive oil, to serve

Preheat the oven to 400°F/200°C.

Place the pumpkin or squash in a large baking sheet and drizzle with half the cooking oil. Bake for 25 minutes, or until soft.

Meanwhile, cook the *maftool* in a pot of boiling water according to the packet instructions. Drain and set aside.

Heat the remaining cooking oil and half the butter in a saucepan. Add the onion and fry over a medium heat for around 10 minutes, until softened. Add the garlic, ginger and the chopped sage and cook for a further 2 minutes. Then add the cooked pumpkin, stock, ½ teaspoon salt and ¼ teaspoon pepper and cook for 5 minutes to bring all the flavors together.

Take the soup off the heat and roughly blend it with a hand-held blender, leaving a few pieces of pumpkin for texture. Taste and adjust the seasoning to your preference.

Finally, make the topping by lightly frying the remaining whole sage leaves in the remaining butter until they are crispy. Stir these through the *maftool* and season with ¼ teaspoon salt.

To serve, ladle the soup into warmed bowls and top with a few spoonfuls of the sage-flavored *maftool*. Finish with a drizzle of extra virgin olive oil.

# Roast cauliflower soup

Cauliflowers are a prized vegetable in the Palestinian kitchen, where their sweet, earthy flavor is celebrated. The most coveted varieties are known as *zahra baladi* (wild flower); they take a year to grow and, when harvested, are the size of my forearm. In Palestinian folklore, they are believed to cure everything from respiratory problems to post-natal pain. In this recipe, cauliflower is cooked into a thick and creamy soup, with just enough warming spice to make you feel as though it is indeed warding off all potential ailments.

Serves 4-6

1 large cauliflower (2 lb./1kg)
2 onions, sliced into half moons
extra virgin olive oil
1½ teaspoons ground cumin
1½ teaspoons ground coriander
sea salt and freshly ground black pepper
2 tablespoons/30g salted butter
4 garlic cloves, crushed

1 large potato (14 oz./400g), skin left on, roughly chopped into 1 in./3cm squares
1 teaspoon ground turmeric
1 quart/1 liter gluten-free vegetable or chicken stock
2 tablespoons flaked almonds, to serve
chopped parsley leaves, to serve

Preheat the oven to 400°F/200°C.

Cut the cauliflower into equal-sized florets and place them, along with any leaves, on a baking sheet with the onions. Drizzle over a few tablespoons of extra virgin olive oil and sprinkle on the cumin and coriander, 1 teaspoon salt and ½ teaspoon pepper. Use your hands to mix everything together, then bake for around 20 minutes, or until the cauliflower is cooked through but still has some bite.

Meanwhile, melt the butter in a large saucepan and sauté the garlic for a few minutes over a low heat. Add the potato, turmeric and stock, cover and cook for 10 minutes, until the potato is soft.

When the cauliflower is done, reserve a few spoons of it for the topping (including leaves, if you have them) and add the remainder to the soup. Simmer everything together for 5 minutes before blitzing with a hand-held blender until it is smooth. Taste and adjust the seasoning.

Toast the flaked almonds in a dry pan over a low heat until they turn golden. When you are ready to serve, ladle the soup into warmed bowls and top with a spoonful of roast cauliflower florets and a scattering of toasted almonds and parsley.

# Red lentil and squash soup with za'atar croutons

Za'atar is a Palestinian spice mix made from wild thyme, sesame and sumac that has a natural affinity with sweet root vegetables. Here it is used to make crunchy, tangy croutons to adorn an aromatic soup of roasted butternut squash and spiced lentils. Roasting the squash intensifies its flavor and sweetness, giving the soup a glorious silky texture that perfectly contrasts with the crispy croutons.

Serves 4

FOR THE SOUP
2 lb./1kg butternut squash, peeled, deseeded and cut into 1 in./3cm pieces
olive oil or any neutral oil
2 onions, finely chopped
4 garlic cloves, crushed
3/4 teaspoon cumin seeds
3/4 teaspoon coriander seeds
1/2 teaspoon ground cinnamon
3/4 cup/160g red lentils, rinsed
3 cups/750ml vegetable or chicken stock
juice of 1/2 lemon
sea salt and freshly ground black pepper

FOR THE TOPPINGS
2 slices of stale bread (I like to use sourdough for taste and texture)
2 tablespoons za'atar
extra virgin olive oil
chopped parsley or cilantro leaves

Preheat the oven to 400°F/200°C.

Place the butternut squash on a baking sheet and drizzle with cooking oil. Toss the chunks so they are evenly coated in the oil, then roast for 20–30 minutes, until they are soft.

Heat 3 tablespoons cooking oil in a large saucepan, add the onions and fry for 10 minutes over a medium heat. Add the garlic, reduce the heat and cook for another few minutes.

Meanwhile, toast the cumin and coriander seeds by stirring them in a dry pan over a low heat for a minute until their aromas are released. Grind the seeds in a mortar and pestle or a spice grinder, then add them and the cinnamon to the saucepan with the softened onions. Fry the spices for a few minutes.

Continued on next page

Add the lentils and 1 quart/1 liter of just-boiled water. Cover and simmer the soup for 10 minutes.

Once the lentils have softened, add the squash, stock, lemon juice, 1 teaspoon salt and ½ teaspoon pepper. Leave to simmer for another 10 minutes.

Once the lentils are fully cooked, take the pan off the heat and blend the soup with a hand-held blender. Taste and adjust the seasoning to your preference.

To make the croutons, roughly chop the bread into 1 in./3cm chunks. Heat 3 tablespoons cooking oil in a frying pan and, once it is very hot, add the bread and sprinkle over the za'atar. Fry the bread, stirring frequently, until it is toasted and crunchy. Place the croutons on a paper towel to soak up any excess oil.

To serve, ladle the soup into warmed bowls, top with the croutons and finish with a drizzle of extra virgin olive oil and a sprinkling of chopped herbs.

# Arugula soup

SHORBAT JARJIR

Wild arugula grows throughout the Palestinian territories, with broad, thick, dark-green leaves that have a much more intensely peppery taste than the varieties commonly found in the West. I like to put them to good use in this fragrant, earthy soup, which feels to me as though it is imbued with vitality from the copious amount of greens cooked into it. As the spicing is kept deliberately light here—because you want to be able to taste the greens—the flavor of the soup will rest largely on the quality of the stock, so opt for the best.

**Serves 4**

2 tablespoons olive oil or any neutral oil
1 medium onion, roughly chopped
4 garlic cloves, crushed
1 teaspoon ground turmeric
½ teaspoon freshly grated nutmeg
¼ teaspoon ground allspice
sea salt and freshly ground black pepper
1 medium potato (about 8 oz./225g), skin left on and chopped
1 quart/1 liter gluten-free chicken stock
8 oz./200g arugula
5 oz./150g spinach
½ cup/30g cilantro, leaves and stalks
Greek yogurt, to serve
2 tablespoons extra virgin olive oil

Heat the cooking oil in a large saucepan. Add the onion and garlic and sauté for 5 minutes over a medium heat. Stir in the spices, 1 teaspoon salt and ½ teaspoon pepper and fry for a couple of minutes more. Then add the potato and stock and simmer for 10 minutes, until the potato is quite soft.

Reserve a handful of arugula and add the remainder to the pan along with the spinach and cilantro. Cook for 10 minutes, then blitz the soup with a hand-held blender until smooth. Taste and adjust the seasoning if you think it needs it.

Pour into warmed soup bowls and finish each with a generous spoonful of Greek yogurt, some of the reserved arugula leaves and the extra virgin olive oil.

# Lentil soup with walnut and cilantro smash

SHORBAT ADAS

An earthy and homely soup, brightened with lemony Swiss chard leaves and an aromatic cilantro, garlic and nut smash. Swiss chard stalks have a flavor similar to celery and are put to good use here by being sautéed for the base of the soup, where they add a mellow sweetness. If Swiss chard isn't readily available, simply substitute it with spinach leaves and add a couple celery sticks instead.

**Serves 4**

FOR THE SOUP
3/4 cup/150g brown or green lentils
1 onion, finely chopped
2 tablespoons olive oil or any neutral oil
1 lb./500g Swiss chard, stalks finely chopped, leaves roughly chopped
2 garlic cloves, crushed
3/4 teaspoon cumin seeds
generous pinch of freshly grated nutmeg
3 cups/750ml gluten-free vegetable or chicken stock

2/3 cup/50g cilantro, leaves and stalks, roughly chopped
juice of 1 lemon
sea salt and freshly ground black pepper
1 tablespoon cornstarch

FOR THE SMASH
1 garlic clove, roughly chopped
3 tablespoons/10g cilantro, leaves and stalks
3 tablespoons/20g walnuts
5 tablespoons extra virgin olive oil, plus more to serve
1 tablespoon lemon juice

Boil the lentils in a saucepan of water for 15 minutes, or until they have just softened. Drain and rinse with warm water. Fry the onion in the cooking oil for 5 minutes over a medium heat. Add the chard stalks and the garlic and fry for another 5 minutes.

Toast the cumin seeds in a dry pan over a medium heat for a minute until the aroma rises, then crush in a mortar and pestle. Add to the onions with the lentils and nutmeg. Add the stock, chard leaves, cilantro, lemon juice, 1 teaspoon salt and a generous grind of pepper. Mix the cornstarch with 1 tablespoon water and add that, too. Cover and cook for 10 minutes.

When the lentils are soft, purée the soup with a hand-held blender, leaving a bit of texture. Taste and adjust the seasoning. Depending on how thick you want your soup, either cook it for a few minutes more over a high heat, or add water to loosen it.

To make the smash, place all the ingredients in a mini food processor or smash them in a large mortar and pestle until you have a rough paste, seasoning with 1/4 teaspoon salt. Spoon a dollop onto each bowl and drizzle with extra virgin olive oil.

# Kale, fennel and noodle soup

RISHTA

This simple, rustic soup is elegantly soothing. It bears a close resemblance to the classic Iranian noodle soup *aash e reshteh*, which leads me to believe that it found its way into the Palestinian kitchen during the time when the Persian empire ruled over the region 2,500 years ago. Whatever its history, it is a soup I make whenever I want to replenish depleted energy levels, or when I want to offer something restorative at the table, as it is packed with greens and healthy legumes. Feel free to substitute the linguine for another pasta, just be sure to adapt the cooking times according to the packet instructions of your noodle.

**Serves 4**

1 onion, finely chopped
2 tablespoons olive oil or any neutral oil
3 garlic cloves, crushed
1 carrot, finely chopped
1 celery stick, finely chopped
1 fennel bulb, finely chopped
1/2 teaspoon fennel seeds
1/2 teaspoon cumin seeds
1/2 teaspoon coriander seeds
1/2 teaspoon dried oregano
sea salt and freshly ground black pepper

about 3/4 cup/140g brown lentils
3 cups/750ml vegetable or chicken stock
2 oz./75g linguine
5 1/2 oz./160g kale, stalks removed, leaves torn
3 tablespoons extra virgin olive oil
juice of 1/2 lemon (optional)

Fry the onion in the cooking oil for about 5 minutes over a medium heat. Add the garlic and fry for another few minutes before adding the chopped vegetables. Stir to coat the vegetables in the oil, then cover and leave them to sweat over a low heat for 10 minutes.

Meanwhile, toast the fennel, cumin and coriander seeds in a dry pan for 1 minute until their aromas are released, then grind them in a mortar and pestle or a spice grinder. Add these to the vegetables, along with the oregano and a generous grind of pepper.

Add the lentils and 1 2/3 cups/400ml just-boiled water, then cover and simmer over a medium heat for 10 minutes. Pour in the stock and cook for another 15 minutes.

Break the strands of linguine into thirds, add them to the pot with 1/2 teaspoon salt and cook for 10 minutes. Finally, add the kale and cook for 5 minutes.

Stir through the extra virgin olive oil, then taste and adjust the seasoning, adding a touch more salt and pepper or a squeeze of lemon juice, as you prefer.

# Freekeh and pinto bean soup

SHORBAT FREEKEH

This rustic soup showcases the smoky Palestinian grain known as freekeh, which has a texture similar to bulgur. According to legend, freekeh was created by accident nearly 2,000 years ago, when a small village was attacked and its crop of young wheat set on fire. After the blaze, instead of throwing the wheat away, the villagers rubbed the burned green grains to remove their charring. When they cooked it, they found to their delight that not only were the grains still edible, but they were absolutely delicious. These days, freekeh is made by picking unripe green wheat and roasting it over wood fires. It imparts a wonderful smoky flavor to dishes and is a popular addition to Palestinian soups.

Serves 4-6

2 tablespoons olive oil  or any neutral oil
1 onion, finely chopped
1 teaspoon coriander seeds
1 teaspoon cumin seeds
1/2 teaspoon ground allspice
2 garlic cloves, crushed
14 oz./400g can of pinto beans, drained and rinsed
1 cup/150g freekeh
2 carrots, peeled and finely chopped
2 celery sticks, finely chopped
4 cups/500ml vegetable or chicken stock
sea salt and freshly ground black pepper
2 tablespoons extra virgin olive oil, plus more to serve
2 tablespoons lemon juice
unflavored yogurt, to serve
3 1/2 tablespoons/15g chives, finely chopped

Heat the cooking oil in a saucepan, add the onion and fry over a medium heat for 10–15 minutes, until soft.

Toast the coriander and cumin seeds by stirring them in a dry pan over a low heat for a minute or so until their aromas are released. Crush them in a mortar and pestle or spice grinder and add to the onion with the allspice and garlic. Fry for another 2 minutes until fragrant.

Add the pinto beans, freekeh, carrots, celery, stock and 2 cups/500ml just-boiled water, cover and simmer for 45 minutes until the freekeh is quite soft. Then season with 1/2 teaspoon pepper and the 2 tablespoons each of extra virgin olive oil and lemon juice. Depending on how salty (or not) your stock was, you may want to add a little more salt. Stir well and cook for 2 minutes.

To serve, ladle into warmed bowls, add generous dollops of unflavored yogurt, a sprinkling of chives and a drizzle of extra virgin olive oil.

# Nablus and Jenin

Sitting cross-legged on a blue plastic tarpaulin, I gently pulled small black olives from their rough branches. Dry red soil crept under my fingernails as I methodically stripped the oil-rich fruits from their leaves. Above me there were men on ladders, black-and-white patterned *keffiyehs* wrapped around their heads to protect them from the blazing afternoon sun. They quietly sang Palestinian folk songs to themselves as they dragged metal rakes through the tree branches, the patter of falling olives providing an ambient percussion to the melodies. There was a calm and confident sense of accomplishment as we piled our gathered olives into yet another basket. It was a rare moment of serenity and peacefulness in the olive groves of Burqin, in the West Bank near Jenin.

Olive trees have been growing in the Fertile Crescent for millennia and today around 80 percent of agricultural land in the West Bank and Gaza is planted with them. Universally regarded as a symbol of peace, olive trees have also come to symbolize Palestinian steadfastness, their roots deeply embedded in a land they have long called home. When uprooted they have also become a symbol of injustice, and Palestinian poetry and artwork is littered with references to the olive tree, often linked to visions of an idyllic Palestinian past.

According to the United Nations, the Israeli military and Israeli settlers have destroyed thousands of olive groves across the OPT and olive farmers remain under threat of being beaten and shot, having their water supplies cut off, or their olive groves torched. Olive trees are routinely bulldozed to make way for the Separation Wall being built around the West Bank, or for the infrastructure required to service Israel's illegal settlements.

But despite these hardships, olive trees remain a source of great joy to Palestinians. The annual olive harvest that takes place in October and November is a key social event in Palestinian culture, an opportunity for several generations to gather together and celebrate the season's harvest. In recent years, they have increasingly been joined by thousands of international volunteers, who attend as a form of solidarity and to provide human protection from any potential acts of violence from Israeli settlers. The festivities and traditions that accompany the weeks of harvesting are seen by many Palestinians as a demonstration of a deep connection to the land, one they do not want to relinquish.

I was visiting the olive groves as a guest of Canaan Fair Trade, a Palestinian social enterprise founded in 2004, which was the first company in the world to export organic, Fair Trade Palestinian olive oil. Canaan works with more than 1,400 Palestinian farmers to produce top-quality extra virgin olive oil, almonds, figs, freekeh and wild foraged ingredients such as capers. It organizes an annual olive harvest festival on the first Friday of November, a time of great feasting

and celebrating, with plenty of food and *dabkeh*, a traditional Palestinian line dance.

I paused from my olive picking to sit with Abu Arrah, one of the workers, who has been helping on this farm for seven years. We rested, leaning against the trees, sipping small cups of sweet, cardamom-infused coffee. "The olive harvest is a time for people to come together and talk to each other," he told me. "We use it as an opportunity to express ourselves. We spend long days here and, as well as sharing our work, we share stories of what is going on in our lives." He looked over to his wife, collecting the coffee cups and placing them back on their tray, preparing to start the next shift of picking. "Our olive harvest gives us beautiful days that gather our family together. It sustains us."

—

Driving into the city of Nablus, the energy shifts sharply from those quiet fields of Jenin to the loud bustle of a town complete with traffic-choked streets and colorful buildings. Walking through the narrow corridors of the market, I passed vendors calling out the virtues of their produce, laughing and joking as hip-swaying Arabic music fell out of shop fronts. Lively and upbeat, the atmosphere was strikingly different from sleepy seaside Akka or perpetually tense Jerusalem. "This is a proper Palestinian city!" declared Raya, with no small amount of pride.

—

Nablus is another of the ancient cities of Palestine and was a center of trade and commerce during the Ottoman era. The food culture here had a great influence in the region, its most famed export being *knafeh*, a sumptuous dessert made from melted Nabulsi cheese sandwiched between layers of crunchy semolina pastry, then doused in a sweet orange blossom or rose syrup. *Knafeh* is an iconic dish that has now spread throughout the Levant and Turkey. Back in Nablus, a team of bakers set the Guinness World Record in 2009 for the largest *knafeh* ever made, weighing in at 3,871 pounds.

The Al Aqsa café is reportedly one of the best *knafeh* joints in town, so we headed straight there. It was only 10.30am, but already hungry crowds were gathered on the roadside around the café, waiting to feast on sticky slices of the freshly made pastry. The air was filled with the scent of melted ghee and toasted semolina and each time a large tray of *knafeh* (around a yard in diameter) came out, it was sliced and distributed in a matter of minutes. I ordered a piece and parked myself on a street corner to savor it. My spoon cracked through the toasted pastry crust and glided through warm, stretchy melted cheese. It was comforting and familiar, a winning combination of sweet with salty. A good start to the day.

We wandered on through the market, stopping every so often to chat to the shopkeepers we met on our way. There is a confidence to the people of Nablus, a place that has kept its distinctly Palestinian identity throughout centuries of foreign rule. I found new culinary discoveries on every corner, feasted on small pockets of toasted flatbread stuffed with cumin-seasoned lamb and sweet warm rotis filled with candied pumpkin jam, speckled with nigella seeds.

Nablus's second most famous export is tahini, a thick paste made from ground roasted sesame seeds, one of the principal ingredients of hummus and also eaten with Palestinian salads and meats. I stopped at the shop of Harab Titi, whose family have sold tahini in the city for a generation. The tahini was creamy and smooth, with a welcome hint of sea salt and a touch of caramel. I bought three large jars and stuffed them into my backpack, looking forward to experimenting with them in the kitchen.

Back on the streets, I spotted a stall on the corner selling hot *taboon* bread; the vendor told us it was baked around the corner and invited us into the tiny underground bakery, hidden below the main thoroughfare. Inside, we watched men rolling out dough and placing it on metal paddles that they slid into a cavernous oven. The bread cooks in a matter of minutes, puffing up like large poppadums, then deflating immediately upon leaving the oven. Known today as Muna's bakery, the space in which it operates has functioned as a bakery for more than 400 years and, standing in the corner of the room watching the rhythmic movements of the bakers, I thought of all

the history that has taken place outside these walls, while here, inside, the simple art of mixing water with flour and leaven in order to sustain people has stayed the same.

—

We moved on to visit Beit al Karama, a women's community and social center in the heart of Nablus's old city. It is run by Fatima Kadumy, a tall and striking woman who initially founded the organisation to provide psychological support for women who had undergone trauma, but now uses it as a social and educational space as well as running cooking classes for visitors who want to learn more about Palestinian cuisine. "Our gatherings are a way of educating women," she told me. "We use food to encourage women to come together; if they need to make a large batch of pickles or jams, for example, they can come and do it in groups, sharing stories of how life is treating them. Creating this safe space for women to meet is important, as it helps them develop a support network for each other."

Fatima moved our conversation into the kitchen where Neda and Rawand, two volunteers for the center, offered to show me how to make *malfouf*, the ever-popular Palestinian dish of stuffed white cabbage rolls filled with ground lamb and rice and poached in a lemony, garlicky broth. The women glided effortlessly between the kitchen stations, showing me how to deftly roll the cabbage leaves and letting me in on

their seasoning secrets ("always use generous amounts of paprika and cumin"). But, half-way through cooking, the water in the building cut off just as we were about to make the sauce to poach the cabbage in, so we took a coffee break and the women retreated to the courtyard to smoke cigarettes. "It happens all the time," Fatima told me. "We are used to it now."

Even though Nablus is in the West Bank and supposedly under Palestinian authority, the Israeli army controls the majority of its water resources. "Most of the water around here is diverted to Israeli settlements in the surrounding area, so it regularly cuts out." Fatima said. "We never know when it will happen and this is one of our biggest challenges." Fortunately, the water came back after an hour and we were able to resume cooking, placing the cabbage in the seasoned broth and preparing a soup made with red lentils to accompany it.

By the time the sun set, our food was ready to eat and we served it in the courtyard; the hot soup, earthy and filling, warmed our bellies as the air around us began to chill.

Water scarcity came up again later that week, when I visited a women's farming co-operative near Anza village. Bassema Barahmeh is the chair of the co-operative, a small group of women who produce maftool, the giant hand-rolled Palestinian couscous, freekeh (green, smoked bulgur wheat) and a za'atar spice rub. Bassema invited me to her house to meet with a group of women from the co-op, a lively, boisterous crew who laugh with the volume and frequency of people who have known each other for many, many years.

I'd come to here to learn how to make maftool, and the women led me to the kitchen where they emptied cracked bulgur wheat into a large bowl, added flour, salt and water and deftly rolled and pounded with their palms until the mixture swelled into plump balls. The speed was astounding, wrists pounding and twisting the flour around the bowl with such ferocity that it didn't take them long to have rolled enough to feed our group. So we moved swiftly on to our accompaniment, a chicken stew cooked in a light broth with chickpeas and flavored with cumin, mint, olive oil and a squeeze of lemon juice.

As the stew bubbled away on the stove, I asked Bassema what life is like as a farmer in the West Bank. "We love to grow our food, just as our families have done for generations," she told me, dipping a spoon into the steaming pot and tasting it for seasoning. "But we don't always have the opportunity. The Israeli army controls the water and the roads around us, and soldiers and settlers can interfere with what we are doing any time they want." She passed the spoon to me, gesturing for me to have a taste, too. "Our lives are simply not in our control." She sprinkled in a generous pinch of salt and gave the pot a good stir. "Apart from how we make our food, of course."

# MAIN COURSES

When I first visited the Palestinian territories, I expected my meals to be dominated by meat— lamb in particular—but in reality vegetables, pulses and grains form the bedrock of most Palestinian food.

At home, meat is used in small amounts to flavor stews, or is mixed with rice to stuff vegetables. In the coastal towns of The Galilee and in the Gaza Strip, fish and seafood also feature prominently.

It's a different story on the streets: succulent kebabs and grilled meats are eaten in roadside cafés or in restaurants throughout Palestinian neighborhoods, filling the air with the sweet scent of roasting meat, ready to be tucked into warm flatbreads, along with salad and pickles. My favorite crowd-pleasing meat recipes are here; they're great for entertaining.

For a colorful and bountiful feast, you can mix and match the vegetarian dishes with salads and *mazzeh* (mezze) dishes from the earlier chapters. There are plenty of recipes that will appeal to everyone, such as juicy eggplants, satisfying chickpeas or veggie feta-spiked *kefte* balls. Palestinian fish dishes—whether fried and smothered in tahini sauce, or flash-grilled and doused with a spicy green salsa—are healthy, easy and delicious. Use fish that is local to you and in season to make your meals more economical and environmentally sound; the fish will be fresher, too.

# Roast eggplant with spiced chickpeas and tomatoes

MUSAKA'A

This dish is etched in my memory forever after a magical moonlit evening spent in the garden of Sumood wa Hurriya. She is a vivacious social organizer involved in the Palestinian local organic food movement, and one of the founders of the Farashe Yoga Center in Ramallah, which runs yoga classes for women in refugee camps. Sumood insisted that I visit her on the evening of a "super full moon," when she gathered a group of her yogi friends and we sat outside, wrapped in scarves under the stars, feasting on her delicious food. I don't know if it was the good company, her non-stop jokes, or the vast moon's luminescent energy, but every morsel Sumood fed us that night in the garden tasted incredible, including this simple yet flavorsome vegetarian dish. It is an easy weekday supper and is best served at room temperature (*musaka'a* actually means 'cold dish' in Arabic). Moonlight al fresco dining optional.

**Serves 4 as part of a spread**

1⅓ lb./600g eggplant (about 2 large ones)
2 tablespoons olive oil or any neutral oil, plus more for the eggplant
sea salt and freshly ground black pepper
1 onion, finely chopped
3 garlic cloves, crushed
14 oz./400g can of plum tomatoes
14 oz./400g can of chickpeas, drained and rinsed
2 teaspoons sugar
¼ teaspoon ground cinnamon
¼ teaspoon ground allspice
½ teaspoon ground cumin
extra virgin olive oil, to serve
chopped cilantro, to serve

Preheat the oven to 400°F/200°C.

Cut the eggplants in half, then into quarters and finally slice them into ¾ in./2.5cm chunks. Place in a baking pan, drizzle with some cooking oil, sprinkle over a pinch of salt and then toss the eggplant to coat. Place in the oven and bake for 20 minutes, or until soft.

Meanwhile, fry the onion in a large saucepan in 2 tablespoons cooking oil until soft and golden (this will take about 15 minutes). Add the garlic and fry for a few minutes before adding the tomatoes, chickpeas, sugar, spices and some salt and pepper. Fill the tomato can up with just-boiled water and add that to the pot, too. Cover and cook for 30 minutes, until the chickpeas are very soft.

Add the eggplant and cook for a final 10 minutes, splashing in more hot water if the dish looks dry.

Leave to cool to room temperature before drizzling over plenty of extra virgin olive oil and scattering with cilantro.

# Eggplant and feta kefte

The Palestinian kitchen is filled with a variety of meat, fish and vegetable *kefte*, which are balls of seasonal ingredients that have been molded, stuffed, baked or fried. This is my interpretation of a vegetarian *kefte*, using the region's ubiquitous eggplants married with fresh, fragrant herbs and tangy white cheese. These are perfect for picnics and keep well for a few days in the fridge.

Serves 4-6

1 lb./600g eggplants (about 2 large ones) chopped into ¼ in./1cm squares
3 tablespoons olive oil or any neutral oil, plus more for the sheet
sea salt and freshly ground black pepper
1⅓ cups/175g bulgur wheat
½ teaspoon cumin seeds
½ teaspoon coriander seeds
1 garlic clove, finely chopped
3 tablespoons/10g mint leaves, finely chopped
3½ tablespoons/15g parsley leaves, finely chopped
6 oz./175g feta cheese, crumbled
⅓ cup/50g sunflower and pumpkin seeds
2 eggs, lightly beaten
finely grated zest of 1 unwaxed lemon

Preheat the oven to 400°F/200°C.

Place the eggplant pieces on a baking sheet and drizzle with the 3 tablespoons cooking oil and ½ teaspoon salt. Use your hands to mix the pieces, then roast for 25 minutes, or until soft. Transfer to a large mixing bowl and leave to cool.

Bring a saucepan of water to the boil, add the bulgur wheat and cook for 15 minutes. Drain, rinse with cold water, drain well again, then add the bulgur to the eggplant.

Preheat the oven to 425°F/220°C, or just increase the temperature if you didn't turn the oven off.

Toast the cumin and coriander seeds by stirring them in a dry pan for a few minutes until their aromas are released, then grind in a mortar and pestle or a spice grinder. Stir into the eggplant and bulgur wheat with all the remaining ingredients, seasoning with ½ teaspoon each salt and pepper.

Oil a baking sheet, then use your hands to mold 12 equal-sized *kefte* and place them on the prepared sheet.

Roast for around 20 minutes, or until the *kefte* are golden all over.

# Upside-down rice with eggplants and peppers

MAQLOUBEH

Being of Iranian descent, I love a good rice cake, and this renowned Palestinian recipe of roasted vegetables and spiced rice is one that I have embraced enthusiastically. *Maqloubeh* means 'upside down' in Arabic and that is exactly how the dish is served, introducing a moment of sweet suspense in the kitchen as you flip the dish out of its cooking pot, hoping it will hold its shape. Traditionally made with chicken, my colorful vegetarian version stands up as a fine main course on its own, but also makes a great accompaniment to grilled meat or fish dishes. Serve with unflavored yogurt, Everyday Palestinian salad and some crunchy pickles (see pages 81 and 64–7).

**Serves 6**

2 medium eggplants, cut into ¾ in./2cm-thick discs
2 red peppers, trimmed and sliced
olive oil or any neutral oil
sea salt
leaves from 2–3 sprigs of thyme
1 garlic bulb, separated into cloves, but not peeled
2 medium tomatoes, thickly sliced
1²/3 cups/300g white basmati rice
¾ teaspoon cumin seeds
¾ teaspoon coriander seeds

½ teaspoon ground cinnamon
½ teaspoon ground allspice
1 teaspoon ground turmeric
2 cups/500ml hot gluten-free vegetable or chicken stock
3 tablespoons/40g salted butter, or 4 tablespoons extra virgin olive oil
1 teaspoon Aleppo pepper (*pul biber*), or other mild chilli, or ½ teaspoon chilli flakes
handful of chopped cilantro leaves, to serve

Preheat the oven to 400°F/200°C.

Place the eggplant and red peppers on 2 separate baking sheets. Drizzle them both with cooking oil, ½ teaspoon salt and thyme leaves, then dot the sheets of peppers with the unpeeled garlic cloves. Transfer both sheets to the oven and bake for 25–30 minutes. After 20 minutes, add the tomatoes to the peppers. At the end of cooking, the vegetables will all be soft.

Meanwhile, rinse the rice in cold water a few times to remove its excess starch (you will know it is ready when the water runs clear), then place it in a large bowl of cold water and leave to soak for 15 minutes. Drain and set aside.

Once the veggies are cooked, set aside to cool. Gently pop the garlic cloves out of their skins.

Toast the cumin and coriander seeds by placing them in a dry pan over a medium heat for a minute or so, stirring until their aromas are released. Grind in a mortar and pestle or spice grinder, then place them in a jug with the remaining spices. Add the hot stock and 3/4 teaspoon salt and stir well.

Melt half the butter or extra virgin olive oil in a large saucepan over a medium heat. Arrange the cooked eggplant so it lines the base of the saucepan neatly (the eggplant slices will be on top once the dish is turned out). Add the tomatoes, roast garlic and peppers on top. Spoon the rice in, then pour over the hot stock and 2/3 cup/150ml just-boiled water. Bring to the boil, then reduce the heat and cover the pan with a few paper towels or a clean dish towel. Place a lid on the pot and cook for 20 minutes. Switch off the heat and leave to rest for 5 minutes before removing the lid and paper towels or dish towel.

Melt the remaining butter—or heat the remaining extra virgin olive oil—in a small saucepan and stir in the Aleppo pepper or other chilli.

To serve, place a large serving platter on top of the saucepan and quickly and deftly invert the pot. Remove the pan to reveal a rice cake with the eggplant on top.

Spoon over the Aleppo pepper butter or oil, then scatter with cilantro to serve.

Pictured on page 140

# Lentil, eggplant and pomegranate stew

RUMMANIYYA

I gravitate towards dishes with pomegranate molasses in them, a remnant no doubt from my childhood where I adored the tangy fruit concentrate so much that I'd sneak into my grandmother's fridge and eat her home-made molasses by the spoonful when no one was looking. *Rumman* means "pomegranate" in Arabic and, when literally translated, this dish means "pomegranatey," highly apt for a recipe sharpened with generous amounts of tart pomegranate juices and then strewn with their ruby seeds. It is a dish that is believed to have originated from the coastal shores of Jaffa, but is also popular in the Gaza Strip, where it was introduced by the Palestinian communities displaced from the northern shores. Traditionally served with flatbreads and olives, I like to eat it with plain steamed rice, too, perfect for soaking up those tart juices.

**Serves 4**

1½ teaspoons cumin seeds
1 teaspoon coriander seeds
1 cup/175g brown lentils
2 large eggplants (around 1 lb./550g total weight), peeled and cut into ¾ in./2cm cubes
⅓–½ cup/80–100ml unsweetened pomegranate molasses
1 tablespoon sumac
sea salt and freshly ground black pepper
extra virgin olive oil
2 banana shallots, finely chopped
olive oil or any neutral oil
5 garlic cloves, crushed
3 tablespoons/10g mint leaves, chopped, plus more to serve
3 tablespoons/10g parsley leaves, chopped, plus more to serve
handful of pomegranate seeds, to serve

Toast the cumin and coriander seeds in a dry pan over a low heat for a minute or so until their aromas are released. Grind them in a mortar and pestle or a spice grinder.

Rinse the lentils in cold water, then place them in a saucepan with the ground spices and 1 quart/1 liter water. Cover and simmer for about 15 minutes, until the lentils begin to soften.

Add the eggplant, ⅓ cup/80ml of the pomegranate molasses, the sumac, 1½ teaspoons salt, ½ teaspoon pepper and 2 tablespoons extra virgin olive oil and simmer for 20 minutes.

Meanwhile, fry the shallots in 2 tablespoons cooking oil until soft and golden, then add the garlic and fry for a few more minutes.

When the lentils and eggplant are quite soft, mash the eggplant into the lentils with the back of a wooden spoon. If the stew starts to dry out, add a touch more water.

Finally, add the fried garlic and shallots and the herbs and simmer for 5 minutes. Taste to adjust the seasoning, adding the extra pomegranate molasses if you think it needs a bit more astringency.

To serve, scatter with pomegranate seeds and strew with some more herbs.

# Comforting spinach and chickpeas

SABANEKH BIL HUMMUS

A soothing and homely stew with a deeply restorative quality, this is a dish I always turn to when I'm in need of comfort. Traditionally the spinach is cooked until its color has darkened and, personally, I prefer the flavor that way, even if it doesn't look as vibrant. This tastes even better after a few hours, so I like to make it ahead of time and serve it with rice or chunks of crusty bread.

**Serves 4**

olive oil or any neutral oil, to fry
1 onion, finely chopped
1 1/2 teaspoons cumin seeds
1 1/2 teaspoons coriander seeds
4 garlic cloves, crushed
1/2 teaspoon ground allspice
generous pinch of freshly grated nutmeg
sea salt and freshly ground black pepper
2 x 14 oz./400g cans of chickpeas, drained and rinsed
2 cups/500ml gluten-free vegetable stock
16 oz./500g spinach, roughly chopped
5 tablespoons lemon juice, or to taste
extra virgin olive oil

Heat 2 tablespoons cooking oil in a large saucepan over a medium heat. Add the onion and fry for around 10 minutes, until it starts to soften.

Toast the cumin and coriander seeds in a dry pan over a low heat for a minute or so, until their aromas are released. Grind the seeds in a mortar and pestle or a spice grinder and add to the onion with the garlic, allspice, nutmeg and 1/2 teaspoon pepper. Fry for a couple of minutes, then add the chickpeas and stock. Cover and simmer for around 30 minutes, or until the chickpeas are plump and soft.

Add the spinach (you may need to add it in batches and wait for each batch to wilt), lemon juice, 1 teaspoon salt and 2 tablespoons extra virgin olive oil. Cook for 5–10 minutes, depending on how you like your spinach, then taste and adjust the seasoning, adding more lemon juice if you want.

# Stuffed cabbage rolls

MALFOUF

If Palestinians can stuff a vegetable, they will, and these thin cigarillo-shaped rolls are one of the most popular in the Palestinian kitchen. I learned how to make them in the kitchen of Beit al Karama, a women's social center in Nablus that promotes Palestinian cooking. Traditionally made with lamb, my version uses lentils instead for a tasty and filling vegetarian dish.

**Serves 8 as part of a spread, or 4 as a stand-alone dish**

FOR THE STUFFING
2/3 cup/120g white basmati rice
1/3 cup/70g brown lentils, rinsed
3 garlic cloves, crushed
1/2 teaspoon ground allspice
1 1/2 teaspoons ground cumin
1 1/2 teaspoons dried oregano
sea salt and freshly ground black pepper
2 tablespoons olive oil or any neutral oil

FOR THE ROLLS
1 large white cabbage (about 2 1/2 lb./1.2kg)
4 garlic cloves, sliced
2 cups/500ml gluten-free vegetable stock
1 1/2 tablespoons dried mint
juice of 1/2 lemon, plus lemon wedges, to serve
4 tablespoons extra virgin olive oil

Rinse the rice until the water runs clear, then place it in a bowl of cold water to soak for 10 minutes.

Cook the lentils in boiling water over a medium heat for 16–18 minutes, until they have softened, but still have some bite. Add the soaked, drained rice for the final 5 minutes of cooking. Drain well and set aside, still in the colander or sieve.

Meanwhile, prepare the cabbage for the rolls. Fill two-thirds of a large saucepan with boiling water. Cut the cabbage in half vertically and then add it to the pan. (Depending on the size of your pan, you may have to do this in 2 batches.) Boil each cabbage half for around 8 minutes, then scoop it out and let it cool for a few minutes before gently peeling off each leaf. If you get toward the center of the cabbage and the leaves are still firm and too hard to peel off, simply pop it back in the water and boil for a few more minutes.

Place the lentils and rice in a large bowl with the crushed garlic, allspice, cumin, oregano, 1 teaspoon salt, 1/2 teaspoon pepper and the cooking oil. Stir well.

Now you are ready to start rolling! Before you begin, here are a few tips to make it easier: don't be tempted to use a lot of stuffing for each leaf, somewhere between 1 teaspoon and 1 tablespoon is enough; and be sure to squeeze the cooked leaves together tightly as you are rolling them, as this helps them to stay together.

Cut the thick stem out of each cabbage leaf. Place a small amount of stuffing in the bottom one-third of each leaf. Fold the sides of the leaf over the stuffing and then roll the leaf away from you, squeezing tightly so the roll stays together. You are aiming for a slim cigar-like shape, but don't expect uniformity with these; depending on the size of your leaf, the size of your stuffed cabbage roll will vary.

Layer the cabbage rolls into a large saucepan, adding the sliced garlic and sprinkling in 1/2 teaspoon pepper as you go. Mix the vegetable stock with 1 teaspoon salt and the dried mint and pour it over the cabbage. Place over a medium heat and bring it to the boil, then reduce the heat, cover and leave to simmer for about 30 minutes, adding the lemon juice halfway through.

To serve, drizzle over the extra virgin olive oil and serve with lemon wedges to squeeze over the rolls.

# Gazan lentils with Swiss chard and tahini

The book that first introduced me to the rich tapestry of Gazan cuisine is *The Gaza Kitchen* by the inimitable Laila El-Haddad and Maggie Schmitt. It's a book that has been crafted with so much heart and insight that it immediately propelled me to my kitchen to bring some of Laila's recipes to life. This creamy and tangy main course is inspired by a recipe in that book and the combination of spicy green chillies with thick tahini is additive. The lentils need to be completely soft and without any bite for this recipe, so cook them until they can easily be smashed with a fork. Serve with warm flatbreads and olives.

**Serves 4–6 as part of a spread, or 2–3 as a stand-alone dish**

1¼ cups/225g brown lentils
2 tablespoons olive oil or any neutral oil
2 bunches of Swiss chard (about 2 lb./1kg), stalks finely chopped, leaves roughly chopped
1 teaspoon cumin seeds
3 garlic cloves, crushed
3 tablespoons tahini
1 green chilli, finely chopped
2 tablespoons lemon juice, plus more to taste
sea salt and freshly ground black pepper
3 tablespoons extra virgin olive oil, plus more to serve
½ teaspoon sumac

Cook the lentils in a large saucepan of simmering water for 30 minutes, or until they are completely soft. Drain, rinse with warm water, then return them to the pan.

Meanwhile, heat the cooking oil in a large saucepan and gently fry the chard stalks for 10–15 minutes, until tender and melting.

Toast the cumin seeds by stirring them in a dry frying pan over a medium heat until their aroma has been released, then grind them in a mortar and pestle or a spice grinder. Add the ground cumin and the garlic to the chard stalks and fry for another few minutes until the garlic has softened. Then add the chard leaves and pour in 7 tablespoons/100ml water. Cover and cook for 5 minutes, until the leaves have just wilted.

When the lentils are ready, add the chard to their pan along with the tahini, chilli, lemon juice, 1½ teaspoons salt and a generous grind of pepper. Add the extra virgin olive oil and stir well. Cook, uncovered, for 5 minutes. Taste and adjust the seasoning and add more lemon juice if you want.

Serve at room temperature or cold, finishing with a drizzle of extra virgin olive oil and the sumac just before serving.

# Brown rice and lentil pilaf with crispy fried onions

MUJADDARA

There is something deeply comforting about this homely dish that is loved throughout the Middle East. This version uses brown rice, which imparts a nutty flavor and adds a welcome bite. Side dishes are essential here, you'll want creamy unflavored yogurt and a flavorsome crunchy salad, either Gazan salad or Everyday Palestinian salad (see pages 85 and 81) would work well.

**Serves 4**

FOR THE PILAF
1¹/3 cups/240g brown basmati rice
sea salt and freshly ground black pepper
1 cup/175g brown lentils, rinsed
1 teaspoon cumin seeds
1 teaspoon coriander seeds
1 teaspoon ground allspice
3/4 teaspoon ground cinnamon

3 tablespoons olive oil or any neutral oil, or 2 tablespoons salted butter

FOR THE TOPPINGS
3 onions, sliced into thin half moons
3 tablespoons flour
sunflower oil, to fry
chopped parsley leaves

Boil the rice with 1 teaspoon salt in a large saucepan of water until it is cooked through. Drain, then return the rice to the saucepan. Meanwhile, place the lentils in a separate saucepan of boiling water and simmer for 15–20 minutes, or until cooked through but still firm. Drain and add to the rice.

Toast the cumin and coriander seeds in a dry pan over a medium heat for a minute or so until their aromas are released. Then grind them in a mortar and pestle and add the remaining spices.

Heat a frying pan with the cooking oil or butter over a medium heat and cook the spices for a few minutes. Pour this fragrant oil over the rice and lentils with 1 teaspoon salt and 3/4 teaspoon pepper. Gently fold the mixture together. Pour over 3 table-spoons/50ml just-boiled water, cover with a clean dish towel or 4 paper towels, then cook for 15 minutes over a medium heat.

Meanwhile, prepare the onions. Sprinkle them with the flour and season with 1 teaspoon salt. Heat a few tablespoons of sunflower oil in a large frying pan and, when it is very hot, add the onions in batches and fry them until they are brown and crispy. Place them on paper towels to soak up the excess oil.

To serve, spoon the crispy onions over the rice and lentils and scatter with the parsley.

# Sea bream with tahini sauce

Tahini sauce and white fish are a marriage made in heaven. This dish is inspired by my trip to Akka, where we sat on the seafront and feasted on the fresh catch of the day, flash-fried, with the rich garlicky-nutty sauce. Feel free to use any firm, local white fish for this—sea bass would be good—and serve with a green salad and some crusty bread, rice or potatoes on the side.

Serves 2

FOR THE SAUCE
1 tablespoon/50g tahini
2 tablespoons lemon juice
2 tablespoons finely chopped parsley leaves, plus more to serve
1 garlic clove, crushed
sea salt and freshly ground black pepper

FOR THE FISH
2 tablespoons flour
2 fillets of sea bream
olive oil or any neutral oil, to fry

Whisk all the sauce ingredients together with 3 tablespoons/50ml water, seasoning with 1/4 teaspoon each salt and pepper, and set aside for the flavors to infuse. Depending on how thick your tahini is, you may need to add a touch more water; you are aiming for a sauce that has the consistency of runny honey.

Dust a plate with the flour and 1/4 teaspoon salt and then roll the fillets of fish in it, coating both sides.

Heat a little cooking oil in a frying pan over a medium heat. When it is hot, add the fish fillets, skin side down, and cook for 3 minutes, or until the skin is crisp. Flip over and cook for 1 minute or so more on the flesh side until just cooked through.

Transfer to a serving plate, spoon over the tahini sauce and sprinkle with chopped parsley. Serve immediately.

# Lemon, cumin and green chilli sea bass

Spice rubs are a common feature of Gazan cooking, and are put to good use in marinating, stuffing and stewing the myriad varieties of fish and seafood that grace their shores. This is a twist on a classic Gazan spice mix, using the same flavors but adapting them into a garlicky marinade and sauce that can be used with any fish or seafood. Serve the sea bass with rice and a green salad.

**Serves 2–4**

2 medium sea bass (around 10 oz./300g each)
2 small mild green chillies, finely chopped
4 garlic cloves, crushed
6 tablespoons lemon juice
finely grated zest of 2 unwaxed lemons
1 teaspoon ground cumin
sea salt and freshly ground black pepper
extra virgin olive oil
¼ cup/15g cilantro, coarse stalks removed, roughly chopped

With a sharp knife, score both sides of the fish with diagonal lines about ¾ in./2cm apart, cutting down to the bone.

Place all the other ingredients, except the oil and cilantro, in a mortar and pestle, seasoning with ¼ teaspoon each salt and pepper, and smash them together until you have a coarse paste. Stir in 2 tablespoons extra virgin olive oil. Using your fingers, smear 1 tablespoon of the paste over each fish on both sides, making sure you get it into the incisions. Divide the cilantro between the fish cavities, then leave to marinate for 10 minutes.

Preheat the grill to medium-high, then place the fish in a baking pan and drizzle over some extra virgin olive oil. Cook under the grill for 12–14 minutes, turning once and drizzling over more extra virgin olive oil when you do, until just cooked through. When you press with your finger on the thickest part, just behind the gills, you should feel the fillet coming away from the bones.

Serve the remaining marinade as if it were a salsa, on the side.

# Za'atar roast salmon
# with garlicky bean mash

I fell in love with za'atar—the aromatic and tangy Palestinian seasoning of wild thyme, sesame seeds and sumac—after my first visit to the West Bank, where I met women's co-operatives in the Anza village who make batches of the spice mix. It has become one of the most-used spices in my store cupboard ever since. This quick and easy recipe is what I tend to use it for most, as its sharp and fragrant flavor works wonderfully for sprucing up salmon fillets, giving you maximum flavor with minimal effort for an easy midweek supper.

Serves 2

2 salmon fillets
2 tablespoons olive oil or any neutral oil
sea salt and freshly ground black pepper
3 tablespoons za'atar
1 garlic clove, crushed

finely grated zest of 1 unwaxed lemon, plus lemon wedges to serve
2 tablespoons/25g salted butter
14 oz./400g can of cannellini beans, drained and rinsed

Preheat the oven to 400°F/200°C.

Place the salmon fillets on a baking sheet, skin side down. Drizzle evenly with the cooking oil and season with 1/2 teaspoon salt and a generous grind of pepper. Spoon over the za'atar, coating as much of the surface of the salmon as you can. Pop the fish into the oven and bake for 11–13 minutes, or until the fillets are just cooked through.

Fry the garlic and lemon zest in the butter for a few minutes over a low heat. Add the beans, 2 tablespoons water, 1/2 teaspoon salt and 1/4 teaspoon pepper. Heat the beans through and then, using a fork or potato masher, roughly mash them. If the mixture looks a bit dry, add a splash more water.

When the fish is ready, transfer each piece to a warmed serving plate with half the mashed beans and serve with lemon wedges. Roast rainbow carrots with herbed yogurt (see page 84) would be a welcome addition, as would a crisp salad.

# Spicy shrimp and tomato stew

ZIBDIYIT GAMBARI

The Gazan playwright and author Ahmed Masoud introduced me to this dish, which embodies the fiery, garlicky and dill-infused cooking of the Gaza Strip. Traditionally baked in a clay pot, I've adapted this recipe for the hob. As varieties of chilli can differ in strength, add them in stages until the sauce has the right level of heat for you.

**Serves 4**

2 tablespoons olive oil or any neutral oil
1 red onion, finely chopped
14 oz./400g can of plum tomatoes
1 teaspoon sugar, or to taste
3/4 teaspoon ground cumin
1/4 teaspoon ground allspice
1/2 teaspoon caraway seeds
sea salt and freshly ground black pepper

3 garlic cloves, crushed
2 tablespoons finely chopped dill
1–2 green chillies, finely chopped, or to taste
2 tablespoons sesame seeds
14 oz./400g raw shrimp, peeled and deveined
extra virgin olive oil
chopped parsley leaves

Heat the cooking oil in a saucepan over a medium heat. Add the onion and fry for about 10 minutes, until softened. Then add the tomatoes, sugar, spices and 1/2 teaspoon each salt and pepper, with 3/4 cup/200ml just-boiled water.

Smash the garlic, dill, chillies and 1/2 teaspoon salt together in a mortar and pestle for a few minutes. This releases the oils from the chillies and herbs and makes them more fragrant. Add to the tomato pan, cover and simmer for 20 minutes over a low heat.

Meanwhile, toast the sesame seeds by placing them in a dry pan and stirring over a medium heat for a few minutes until they turn golden brown. Remove from the pan and set aside.

When the sauce is ready, taste and adjust the seasoning (you may want to add a pinch more sugar or a bit more chilli). Finally, add the shrimp—making sure they are submerged and turning them if necessary—cooking for about 2 minutes, or until they have just turned pink and are cooked through.

To serve, drizzle with a generous amount of extra virgin olive oil and scatter with the sesame seeds and chopped parsley.

# Spiced fish pilaf with caramelized onions

SAYADIEH

This comforting rice pilaf epitomizes the soothing side of the Palestinian kitchen. It is a dish that is popular all along the region's coast, where each village and town has their unique version. I first learnt how to make it in the kitchen of Hajji Monira, a women's community activist in Haifa (see page 71). You can use any firm local white fish of your choice, such as hake. I like to serve this with a crunchy salad, such as Donyana salad or Gaza salad (see pages 91 and 85).

Serves 4

FOR THE TARATOR SAUCE
3 teaspoons/75g tahini
3 tablespoons lemon juice, or to taste
1/3 cup/25g parsley leaves, finely chopped
1/2 teaspoon sea salt

FOR THE FISH AND MARINADE
1½ lb./700g skinned white fish fillets (cod, pollack, hake or monkfish all work well), cut into 2 in./5cm chunks
finely grated zest of 1 unwaxed lemon
1 teaspoon ground cumin
1 teaspoon paprika
3 tablespoons flour
sea salt and freshly ground black pepper
2 tablespoons olive oil or any neutral oil

FOR THE RICE
1 tablespoon/20g salted butter
2 tablespoons olive oil or any neutral oil
2 onions, finely sliced into half moons
1 1/3 cups/250g white basmati rice
1 1/2 teaspoons cumin seeds
1 1/2 teaspoons coriander seeds
3 garlic cloves, crushed
1/4 teaspoon ground turmeric
1/2 teaspoon ground allspice
4 cups/500ml vegetable stock
2 1/2 tablespoons/20g pine nuts
sumac, to serve

Make the tarator sauce by mixing all the ingredients together with 7 tablespoons/100ml water. As tahini brands can vary, add more water or lemon juice to suit your preference. You are aiming for the consistency of thick runny honey.

Place the fish in a bowl with all the marinade ingredients, apart from the oil, with 1 teaspoon salt and 1/4 teaspoon pepper. Mix, cover and leave to marinate while you prepare the rice.

Melt the butter and oil for the rice in a large saucepan, add the onions and fry them over a medium-low heat for about 20 minutes, stirring occasionally, until they are soft and brown.

Meanwhile, rinse the rice until the water runs clear, then place it in a large bowl of cold water to soak for 15 minutes. Drain and set aside.

Toast the cumin and coriander seeds by placing them in a small dry saucepan over a medium heat and stirring for 1 minute until their aromas have been released, then grind the spices in a mortar and pestle or a spice grinder.

When the onions are ready, add the crushed garlic and fry for 2 minutes. Now add the drained rice, all the spices, 1 teaspoon salt and some pepper to the pan and stir well. Pour in the stock, bring to the boil, then cover, reduce the heat to low and cook the rice for 15 minutes. Take it off the heat and let it rest for 10 minutes.

Toast the pine nuts by placing them in a small dry saucepan for a minute or so, stirring until they are golden.

To cook the fish, heat the 2 tablespoons cooking oil in a frying pan and, when it is very hot, add some of the fish pieces. Fry them for 7–8 minutes, turning occasionally, until they are golden brown on both sides. Cook them in batches so you don't overcrowd the pan and the oil stays hot. Place the cooked fish on a paper towel to soak up any excess oil.

To serve, use a fork to fluff up the rice grains and transfer the pilaf to a warmed serving platter. Place the fish pieces on top, then spoon over the tarator sauce. Finish with a sprinkling of pine nuts and a generous smattering of sumac.

# Akkawi spiced crispy squid

There is an abundance of delicious seafood in the coastal town of Akka in northern Galilee, and it was here that I first enjoyed this delightful dish of Palestinian spiced calamari, served with a tahini and parsley dipping sauce. This is a supremely flexible recipe, so feel free to adjust the spicing as you prefer. I like to use baby squid: I find them more tender than large squid and they are easily found in the frozen sections of most big supermarkets. In order to keep a lovely soft and springy texture, be careful not to overcrowd the pan when frying them, as that reduces the temperature of the oil and affects the cooking process. Think 'hot and fast', and cook the squid in batches.

**Serves 6 as part of a spread, or 2 as a stand-alone dish**

1 lb./500g baby squid, cleaned and cut into 3/4 in./2cm-thick rings (plus tentacles, if possible)
5 tablespoons flour
5 tablespoons cornstarch
3 teaspoons Aleppo pepper (*pul biber*), or 1 1/2 teaspoons chilli flakes
3 teaspoons ground cumin
1 teaspoon ground allspice
sea salt and freshly ground black pepper
sunflower or any neutral oil, to fry
lemon wedges, to serve

Rinse the squid, then pat dry with paper towels.

Mix both flours, the spices, 1 teaspoon salt and 1/2 teaspoon pepper in a zip-top plastic bag or plastic container. Drop the squid into this seasoned flour, zip up the bag or put the lid on, then give it all a good shake.

Pour enough oil into a large frying pan to fill it a couple of inches/centimeters deep. Heat the oil until it's very hot. Cover a large dinner plate with a few paper towels.

Carefully drop the squid pieces into the hot oil in batches, being careful not to overcrowd the pan. Flip them over once they're golden on one side, so they become an even color all over. Depending on how thick each piece is, they'll take no more than 35–45 seconds in total. Lift the squid out with a slotted spoon and place them on the paper towels to soak up any excess oil. Working fast, cook the remaining squid.

Serve immediately, with lemon wedges and salt to sprinkle on top.

# Gaza

Ahmed tore a large handful of dill from the tangle of green herbs on his kitchen counter and began rhythmically to roll the green fronds between his palms. The room filled with the sweet scent of anise. "I sniffed my hands the other day," Ahmed said, glancing down at them, "and I realized I smelled like my mum. She always told us to rub dill and garlic together with the flats of our palms when we were preparing it. She insisted it made the food taste better." Ahmed brought his right hand to the tip of his nose and sniffed gently. He smiled. "This, for me, is the smell of Gaza."

Gazan cuisine is known for its abundant use of dill: its fresh leaves are chopped into salads and stuffed into the cavities of fish, and its seeds are ground and added by the spoonful to soups and stews. Dill sits alongside garlic and chillies to form a holy trinity of Gazan cuisine, giving it a distinct flavor palette that sets it apart from other Palestinian food.

With a strong emphasis on fish and seafood, traditional Gazan dishes tend to veer toward the sharper end of the culinary spectrum, using tart pomegranate juice, sharp lemons, sour plums and tangy sumac to give dishes the requisite acidity. Even the staple of tahini is amplified in Gaza into a special red tahini made from roasted sesame seeds, giving it a more pronounced and nutty flavor. It is used in stews such as *sumagiyya*. The food of Gaza is intense. Just like its recent political history.

I was in Ahmed's kitchen—in a leafy suburb of north London—to learn more about Gaza, a place I was sadly unable to visit. Since 2007, the Gaza Strip has been closed to the outside world, held under siege by the Israeli government, and all movement of goods and people in and out is controlled by Israeli authorities. More than two million people live in the Gaza Strip, a small piece of land just 25 mi./40km long and 5½ mi./9km wide, making it one of the most densely populated places on earth. Surrounded by a concrete and steel wall built by Israel, Palestinians in Gaza are trapped in what United Nations officials have called "the world's largest prison."

The siege affects all aspects of life. Today, 80 percent of Gazans rely on food aid to survive and malnutrition is rife. Israel has banned foreign trade and food supplies are restricted. The list of goods allowed in is so punitive that even pasta, lentils, chocolate, coffee, nappies and school books have been denied. Essential medical kit and medicines are restricted, as are building materials such as cement and wood.

On top of this, Gazans have endured—at the time of writing—three major rounds of hostilities, killing thousands of civilians and destroying homes and infrastructure. The lack of materials to maintain or repair what's left has led to 96 percent of Gaza's water being unfit for human consumption, according to the United Nations, and crippling electricity shortages, sometimes amounting to just a few hours each day.

The situation in Gaza has led to international outrage from across the political spectrum. Former president Jimmy Carter noted most poignantly: "The citizens of Gaza are treated more like animals than human beings. Never before in history has a large community been savaged by bombs and missiles and then deprived of the means to repair itself."

—

As I couldn't go to Gaza in person, I traveled there through the kitchens of Gazans in the diaspora. Ahmed was one of my most charming hosts, a playwright and novelist who was born in the Jabalia camp in the north of the Gaza Strip. As we prepared *zibdiyit gambari*, a Gazan speciality of shrimp and tomato baked in a clay pot, his young daughter ran in and out of the kitchen asking to be involved, so we divided the tasks between us, Ahmed grating onion for the stew and his daughter and I chopping vegetables for the accompanying salad.

"Fish is everything in Gaza," Ahmed said, dropping plump raw shrimp into a cast-iron pot. "It was our main food source. Especially sardines, there were so many when I was growing up. We'd barbecue them on the beach, make them into *kibbeh*, bake them, fry them... They were cheap and plentiful."

The shrimp sizzled in the pan and Ahmed watched them intently, waiting for that brief moment when their color changes from translucent gray to pale pink, before hastily transferring them to a plate with a slotted spoon. "I come from a large fishing family," he continued, returning to the pot to pour in generous glugs of oil. "My grandfather had 10 sons and they all were fishermen. He was known for eating raw fish and I swear it was good for him as he lived to 110 and had a perfect memory right up to when he died!"

As the oil began to sizzle, Ahmed tipped onions into the pan, stirring with his wooden spoon to coat the pieces with a slick of oil. "But Gaza's fishing industry is struggling now," he continued. "It's not how it used to be before the siege. Today, fishermen are only allowed to fish in a small area close to the shore due to restrictions placed on them. If they go beyond the permitted fishing zone, they can be shot at by Israeli soldiers."

—

The challenges to Gaza's fragmenting fishing industry encompass more than just these restrictions. Omar Gharib, a Gazan blogger and journalist, told me that much of Gaza's water has become contaminated with sewage due to its war-damaged infrastructure. "As the Israeli authorities don't allow fishermen to fish further out to sea in cleaner waters, the fish people collect these days is questionable in terms of food safety. I avoid it."

Omar is speaking to me via Skype from Gaza City, giving me the lowdown on his favorite Palestinian dishes and how to prepare them. Like many others around the world, spending time in the kitchen is how

Omar relaxes, and he finds the meditative quality of cooking a vehicle through which he can escape the challenges of everyday life in Gaza. He talked me through *maqloubeh*, a bountiful feast dish of an upside-down rice cake, layered with eggplant and peppers, and also about his experiments with international cuisine. "I am obsessed with Pakistani food," he tells me excitedly, upon hearing my father was born there. "I love everything about it!"

But even in the kitchen, Omar can't escape his concerns. "There has been a spike in cancer rates that no one talks about," he told me, sighing heavily. "Our land is filled with the remnants of tons and tons of artillery and missiles and bombs... how do you think that is affecting the soil?"

In 2009, Israel used white phosphorus against Gazans during the Operation Cast Lead hostilities, and Omar fears the ongoing damage of these chemical weapons is affecting Gaza's produce. "No matter how much you clean the vegetables, you always wonder, is this really clean? Or is this carrot going to give me cancer?"

Nevertheless, many of Omar's fondest memories revolve around food and, in particular, the time he would spend in his grandmother's kitchen, a place where he'd seek solace at the end of his school day, sampling her food as she was cooking. "I was in my grandmother's kitchen the first time I remember Gaza being bombed," he told me. "I was a kid and I remember hearing the helicopters above us. It was the first time I'd heard such a roar and it was deafening, I didn't know what was happening. I started panicking and I kept telling my grandmother: 'We need to leave, we need to leave the kitchen!' And we started hearing all of these bombs and explosions around us." Omar paused for a moment and I realized I was holding my breath. I exhaled. "But you know what?" he continued. "My grandmother did not flinch. She said, 'I'm cooking and if I leave now everything will be ruined. I'm not going anywhere.' She was making a dish with cooked yogurt and cornstarch, a dish that requires stirring the whole time otherwise it will burn or separate. She was determined, she had started cooking and she wanted to finish it. It was the first time I realized that fear doesn't have to control us."

It is this realization that Omar believes makes Gazans so resilient. "People in Gaza really love life," he told me. "We don't take life for granted. If there is darkness, we manage to find some light; if there is ugliness, we manage to find some beauty; if there is despair, we find or create some hope. It is something that we have developed, like a skill. This is the image of Gaza I would like people to know about. It's not just a place of death and destruction and bombs and dying and Hamas and Fatah and Israel and war and borders, we are not only that. We are two million people, just humans like everyone else in the world, waking up to life every day and looking for the chance to be happy."

# Warm maftool salad
# with za'atar chicken

*Maftool* is a plump and round Palestinian couscous made from wheat flour. Sometimes labeled as "giant couscous" in the West, it is a wonderfully versatile ingredient with a texture similar to pasta, so it keeps its bite and shape when cooked. The word *maftool* means "hand-rolled" in Arabic and, today, Palestinian women prepare it exactly as their grandmothers did, working in small groups to crack and roll the wheat with their hands before placing it out under the hot sun to dry. This flavorsome recipe is my favorite way of using this ancient grain food; it is a dish that sings with the bright flavors of tangy sumac and aromatic fresh herbs. I prefer to use wholewheat *maftool*, as it gives a slightly nuttier taste and texture, but if you are using regular *maftool*, simply reduce the volume of cooking liquid a little.

**Serves 4**

FOR THE CHICKEN
4 chicken legs on the bone
   (thigh and drumstick
   attached), skin on
4 tablespoons extra virgin
   olive oil
2 garlic cloves, crushed
4 tablespoons za'atar
juice of 1 lime
sea salt and freshly ground
   black pepper

FOR THE MAFTOOL SALAD
2 onions, finely chopped
olive oil or any neutral oil
4 garlic cloves, crushed
1/2 teaspoon ground allspice
1 1/2 cups/250g wholewheat
   *maftool*
2 cups/500ml chicken stock
1/3 lb./150g green beans,
   trimmed
1 tablespoon sumac
juice of 1 lemon
3 oz./100g arugula
3 1/2 tablespoons/15g parsley
   leaves, finely chopped
3 1/2 tablespoons/15g mint
   leaves, finely chopped
2 tablespoons extra virgin
   olive oil

Using a sharp knife, slash the thigh of each chicken leg diagonally in 3–4 places, cutting down to the bone. Place the chicken in a bowl or plastic container, drizzle over the extra virgin olive oil, garlic, za'atar and lime juice and season with 1 1/2 teaspoons salt and 1/2 teaspoon pepper. With your hands, rub the marinade into the chicken, then cover and leave in the fridge for at least 2 hours, or up to 6 hours, for the flavors to infuse the meat.

When you are ready to cook, preheat the oven to 400°F/200°C. Place the chicken legs in a roasting pan and bake for around 35 minutes, or until the juices from the chicken run clear when pierced at their thickest part.

Meanwhile, fry the onions in 2 tablespoons cooking oil for 15 minutes, until they are soft. Add the garlic and allspice and fry for a further 2 minutes. Then pour in the *maftool*, stock and

7 tablespoons/100ml water and stir well. Cover and simmer for 20 minutes, until the *maftool* is soft and all the cooking liquid has evaporated. As varieties of *maftool* can vary, check on it after 15 minutes and splash in a touch more water if the pan dries out before the grains are ready.

Chop the green beans into ½-in./4cm-long pieces. Bring a saucepan of water to the boil and cook the beans until they are just tender but still have some bite; depending on the variety, this can take 3–6 minutes. Drain well.

When the *maftool* has cooled a little, transfer to a serving bowl and add the sumac, lemon juice, green beans, arugula, parsley, mint and extra virgin olive oil, stirring in 1 teaspoon salt and ½ teaspoon pepper. Taste and adjust the seasoning as you like.

When the chicken has cooked, leave it to rest for 5 minutes before serving it with the *maftool* salad, spooning the chicken juices over each leg just before you tuck in.

Pictured on page 170

# Roast chicken stuffed with raisins and pine nuts

DJAJ MAHSHI

Roast chicken is a mainstay in my house, so when I heard there was a Palestinian version stuffed with aromatic rice and dotted with dried fruits and nuts, I had to try it. This delights and soothes in equal measure, with its warming flavors of cinnamon and allspice. It originated from The Galilee and is often served there on special occasions, such as at Easter or Christmas. It is so straightforward to make and delicious, I'm sure it will become a regular dish in your house, too, once you try it.

**Serves 4–6**

**FOR THE CHICKEN AND MARINADE**
3¼ lb./1.5kg whole chicken
3 tablespoons extra virgin olive oil
1 teaspoon sumac
½ teaspoon ground allspice
juice of ½ lemon
3 garlic cloves, crushed
sea salt and freshly ground black pepper

**FOR THE STUFFING**
2 tablespoons olive oil or any neutral oil
½ onion, finely chopped
1 garlic clove, crushed
½ teaspoon ground allspice
½ teaspoon ground cinnamon
3 tablespoons/25g pine nuts
2½ tablespoons/25g raisins
¼ cup/45g white basmati rice
1 cup/250ml gluten-free chicken stock

Place the chicken on a baking pan. Combine the marinade ingredients in a bowl, seasoning with 1½ teaspoons salt and ½ teaspoon pepper, then pour it all over the chicken, making sure to rub some inside the cavity. Cover with plastic wrap, then place in the fridge for at least 2 hours, or overnight.

Make the stuffing by heating the cooking oil in a pan, then frying the onion over a medium-low heat for 10 minutes until soft. Add the garlic, spices, ¼ teaspoon salt and ½ teaspoon pepper and cook for a few more minutes. Then add the pine nuts and raisins, cooking for a minute or so until the nuts have slightly browned. Add the rice and stock, place a lid on the pot and cook for 10 minutes until the rice has absorbed the liquid.

Take the chicken out of the fridge about 20 minutes before you cook it so that it returns to room temperature. Preheat the oven to 350°F/180°C. Stuff the rice mixture into the cavity, then tie the chicken legs together with kitchen string to keep the stuffing in place.

Roast for 1 hour 20 minutes, basting after about 1 hour to stop it drying out, or until the juices run clear when the bird is pierced with a sharp knife down to the bone between leg and body. Cover with foil and let it rest for 10 minutes before carving.

# Spiced chicken with dried lime pilaf

MASHBOUS

I spent a magical afternoon in the kitchen of Samia Botmeh, an economist at Birzeit university just outside Ramallah, who guided me through this fragrant rice pilaf that originates from the countries of the Gulf but is now eaten across Palestinian communities. As we cooked, we were enveloped in the wondrous aroma of dried limes that give the dish its distinctive taste. There isn't a substitute for their earthy scent or bitter, citrusy flavor, so it is worth tracking them down online or in Middle Eastern grocery stores. Serve this pilaf with unflavored yogurt and a crunchy salad.

**Serves 4**

3/4 teaspoon coriander seeds
3/4 teaspoon cumin seeds
1/4 teaspoon fenugreek seeds
seeds from 3 cardamom pods
2 dried limes
1/2 teaspoon ground turmeric
1/2 teaspoon ground allspice
1 whole chicken, about 3 lb./1.4kg, cut into 8 pieces, skin on

sea salt and freshly ground black pepper
5 tablespoons olive oil or any neutral oil
1 onion, finely chopped
3 garlic cloves, crushed
1 1/3 cups/250g white basmati rice
1 carrot, finely grated
1/3 cup/50g pine nuts
chopped parsley leaves

Prepare the spice mix by toasting the coriander, cumin, fenugreek and cardamom seeds in a small pan for 1 minute, until their aromas are released. Then grind the spices with the dried limes in a spice grinder and mix with the turmeric and allspice.

Place the chicken in a large bowl. Add half the spice mixture with 1 1/2 teaspoons salt, 1/2 teaspoon pepper and 2 tablespoons of the cooking oil. Using your hands, rub the spices into the chicken, ensuring it is evenly covered on all sides.

Heat another 2 tablespoons cooking oil in a large saucepan over a medium-high heat. When the oil is hot, add the chicken and fry until browned on all sides. Set aside.

Add the onion to the pot and cook for 10 minutes, until soft. Add the garlic and cook for a further few minutes. Wash the rice in several changes of cold water until the water runs clear, then drain and add to the pot with 2 cups/500ml just-boiled water, the carrot and the remaining spice mix. Scrape the base of the pan so all the juices and spices are dispersed. Add 1/2 teaspoon salt, then place the chicken on top. Cover and cook for 35 minutes over a low heat. Take off the heat and leave for 5 minutes.

Heat the remaining 1 tablespoon oil in a pan and add the pine nuts. Cook until they have toasted, then place on a paper towel to drain. Sprinkle the pilaf with pine nuts and parsley to serve.

# Chicken shawarma

Serve these juicy, lemony chicken pieces in warm flatbreads with some tahini sauce, crunchy pickles and a few slices of fresh tomato and cucumber. If you don't have a grill pan, you can also cook them under the broiler preheated to a medium setting.

**Serves 4**

1¾ lb./800g skinless chicken thigh fillets, cut into ¾ in./2cm chunks
finely grated zest and juice of 1 unwaxed lemon
1 garlic clove, crushed
¼ teaspoon ground turmeric

½ teaspoon ground allspice
½ teaspoon ground cumin
3 tablespoons olive oil or any neutral oil
sea salt and freshly ground black pepper

Place the chicken in a large bowl and add all the ingredients, seasoning with 1 teaspoon salt and ½ teaspoon pepper. Mix well, then cover and marinate in the fridge for at least 2 hours.

When you are ready to cook, place a large ridged grill pan over a medium-high heat.

When the pan is hot, place the chicken on it and cook for around 3 minutes on each side until the pieces are just cooked through. Transfer to a plate, cover with foil and leave to rest for a few minutes before serving.

# Roast chicken with sumac and red onions

MUSSAKHAN

*Mussakhan* is a classic Palestinian dish eaten in villages throughout the region. Traditionally the meat is laid out on a giant piece of bread with the flavorsome roasting juices poured over it, so that they seep into the dough. This platter is then placed on the table for everyone to pull off sections of bread and chicken: a wonderful sharing meal. As it can be challenging to find such large pieces of flatbread in most shops, I've suggested using individual naan breads instead... but, of course, if you can, seek out traditional sheets of Arabic *taboon* bread from Middle Eastern stores. If you are avoiding gluten, the chicken is just as delicious on its own, or served with rice or a salad.

**Serves 4**

2 lb./1kg chicken thighs and drumsticks, skin on
3 tablespoons extra virgin olive oil, plus more to serve
1/2 teaspoon ground cumin
1/2 teaspoon ground allspice
1/4 teaspoon ground cinnamon
1 1/2 tablespoons sumac, plus more to dust
juice of 1 lemon
4 garlic cloves, crushed
sea salt and freshly ground black pepper
2 large red onions (about 1 lb./500g), finely sliced into half-moons
2 tablespoons pine nuts
1 tablespoon olive oil or any neutral oil
naan or Arabic *taboon* bread, to serve
chopped parsley leaves

Slash the flesh of each piece of chicken diagonally a few times, around 3/4 inch/2cm apart, and then place the meat in a large bowl or plastic container.

Pour over the extra virgin olive oil, spices, lemon juice, garlic, 1 1/2 teaspoons salt and 1/4 teaspoon pepper and rub this into the meat. Add the red onions and toss everything together well. Cover and leave to marinate in the fridge for 1–3 hours.

When you are ready to cook the chicken, preheat the oven to 375°F/190°C.

Transfer the meat to a baking pan and roast for about 35 minutes, or until the chicken juices run clear when pierced at their thickest part. Once the chicken is cooked, cover in foil and leave to rest while you prepare the toppings.

Fry the pine nuts in the cooking oil for a minute or so until they turn golden brown, then tip onto a paper towel to drain.

To serve, toast the naan or *taboon* bread and then place the chicken and red onion on top. Finish with a smattering of pine nuts, sumac and chopped parsley. Drizzle over any remaining roasting juices so they soak into the bread, then sprinkle over a little more extra virgin olive oil.

# Layered chicken and flatbread feast with yogurt and chickpeas

FATTEH DJAJ

*Fatteh* means 'crushed' in Arabic, and is the name given to a family of dishes that use torn-up shards of toasted, crushed flatbread as their base. These are layered with meat, vegetables, chickpeas and yogurt or tomato sauce. There are innumerable varieties found throughout the region, but this is my favorite, probably because I'm a sucker for roast chicken in all its forms. This is a great dish to serve when you have guests, as all the elements can be made ahead of time and assembled at the last minute. (It is also a very useful way to enjoy leftover roast chicken or turkey.)

**Serves 4-6**

### FOR THE CHICKEN
1 whole chicken, about 3¼ lb./1.5kg, cut into 8 pieces, skin on
4 tablespoons olive oil or any neutral oil
juice of 1 lemon
1 tablespoon ground allspice
1 teaspoon ground cumin
4 garlic cloves, crushed
sea salt and freshly ground black pepper
7 oz./200g Arabic flatbreads (see page 41 for home-made), or pita breads
14 oz./400g can of chickpeas, drained and rinsed

### FOR THE SAUCE
3/4 cup/250g unflavored Greek yogurt
3 tablespoons/50g tahini
1 garlic clove, crushed

### FOR THE TOPPINGS
1 tablespoon/10g salted butter
1/4 cup/30g pine nuts
3 tablespoons/15g chopped parsley leaves
1 1/2 tablespoons sumac
handful of pomegranate seeds (optional)
extra virgin olive oil

Preheat the oven to 350°F/180°C.

Place the chicken in a large roasting pan and pour over the cooking oil, lemon juice, spices, garlic, 1 1/2 teaspoons salt and 1/2 teaspoon pepper. Use your hands to rub the marinade all over the chicken, then place the pan in the oven and roast for about 40 minutes, or until the juices run clear when the chicken pieces are pierced at their thickest part.

Remove the chicken from the pan and leave on a plate to cool. Add 2/3 cup/150ml hot water to the pan and use a spoon to scrape up and mix in any chicken juices and bits that have stuck to the pan. Pour this gravy into a bowl and set aside. While the chicken is cooling, prepare the other elements of the dish.

Make the yogurt sauce by mixing all the ingredients in a bowl with 3 tablespoons/50ml water, 1/2 teaspoon salt and 1/4 teaspoon pepper.

Then cut the flatbreads into thin shards around ¾ in./2cm wide and place them on a sheet in the hot oven for around 10 minutes until they have toasted and are crisp. Finally, melt the butter in a small pan and fry the pine nuts until they are just golden brown. Tip onto a paper towel to absorb the excess butter, if you like.

Once the chicken has cooled and you are ready to assemble the dish, shred the meat from the bones and reheat the gravy.

Place the toasted bread on a serving platter. Add the shredded chicken, followed by the chickpeas, then pour over the gravy, making sure you sprinkle it evenly over the bread. Add the yogurt sauce in an even layer. Finish with the fried pine nuts, chopped parsley, sumac and pomegranate seeds, if using, then drizzle with extra virgin olive oil to serve.

# Gazan beef, chickpeas and Swiss chard

SUMAGIYYA

This sharp and tangy stew is one of the signature dishes of Gaza City and is another recipe adapted from Laila El-Haddad and Maggie Schmitt's excellent book *The Gaza Kitchen*. Traditionally made with dill seeds and the roasted red tahini of the city, my version uses caraway seeds and toasted sesame oil, both more readily available in Western supermarkets. Of course, if you happen to come across the former ingredients, don't hesitate to use them for a more authentic version. In Gaza this is often served at room temperature with warm bread. The accompaniments are up to you; I like it with steamed rice or—if I need something a little more comforting—a generous portion of creamy mashed potato. This tastes even better the next day, so is a great make-ahead dish.

**Serves 4**

2 tablespoons olive oil or any neutral oil
1 onion, finely chopped
4 garlic cloves, crushed
1 lb./500g good-quality stewing beef (I like shin or chuck), cut into 2 in./5cm pieces
2 tablespoons cornstarch
1 teaspoon ground coriander
1 teaspoon ground allspice
1 teaspoon caraway seeds
14 oz./400g can of chickpeas, drained and rinsed
1 tablespoon tomato purée
2 cups/500ml gluten-free chicken stock
sea salt and freshly ground black pepper
1 tablespoon sumac
2 tablespoons tahini
1 tablespoon toasted sesame oil
1/4 teaspoon chilli flakes
2 tablespoons unsweetened pomegranate molasses
2 large bunches of Swiss chard or spinach, roughly chopped (about 1 lb./500g total weight)
1 green chilli, finely chopped

Heat the cooking oil in a large saucepan, add the onion and fry over a medium heat for 10 minutes. Add the garlic and cook for another 2 minutes.

Dust the beef with the cornstarch and then add it to the pot, searing well on all sides. Add the coriander, allspice and caraway seeds and fry for 1 minute before adding the chickpeas, tomato purée and chicken stock. Stir well. If the meat isn't covered, pour in just-boiled water until it is. Season with a generous grind of pepper, then cover with the lid and simmer over a medium-low heat for around 1 1/2 hours, or until the meat is completely tender.

When the meat is ready, add the sumac, tahini, toasted sesame oil, chilli flakes, pomegranate molasses and 1 teaspoon salt. Stir well until you have a creamy sauce. Then add the chard or spinach and green chilli and cook for a final 5 minutes.

Taste and adjust the seasoning, then leave to rest and let the flavors come together for 5–10 minutes, before serving with warm bread, steamed rice or creamy mashed potatoes.

# Bedouin lamb with kashk and spiced rice

MANSAF

*Mansaf* is a celebratory dish, often served at Palestinian weddings and for major feasts. Traditionally the rice and meat is layered on flatbreads and placed in a large platter in the midst of assembled guests. Each uses their right hand to tear off some bread to pick up the rice and lamb with. Eating in this communal way is one of the joys of *mansaf* and it was how I first ate it when community organizer Jamal Juma' (see page 109) cooked it for me in Ramallah. Of course, these days *mansaf* is often eaten with a fork and spoon, and this way it will still be a feast dish to treasure. *Kashk* is a type of fermented whey that has a pungent, umami flavor and a taste with some affinity to a strong goat's cheese. You can find it in Persian grocery stores or online. Choose the liquid variety sometimes (confusingly) labeled "Iranian sauce." Ask your butcher to prepare the lamb and, when you get home, go through it again and trim off excess fat.

**Serves 4-6**

olive oil or any neutral oil
2 lb./1kg lamb shoulder on the bone, cut into 3 in./8cm chunks and trimmed of fat
4 garlic cloves, crushed
3/4 teaspoon cumin seeds
3/4 teaspoon coriander seeds
1/2 teaspoon ground turmeric
1/2 teaspoon ground allspice
1/4 teaspoon ground cinnamon
sea salt and freshly ground black pepper
1 2/3 cups/300g white basmati rice
3/4 cup/200g *kashk*
3/4 cup/200g Greek yogurt

1 egg, lightly beaten
14 oz./400g can of chickpeas, rinsed and drained
pinch of saffron strands
pinch of sugar
2 tablespoons/30g salted butter
seeds from 2 cardamom pods, crushed
1 Arabic *taboon* bread, or 2 white pita breads, cut into 3/4 in./2cm-thick shards
1/3 cup/40g pine nuts
handful of parsley leaves, chopped
sumac, to serve

Heat 1 tablespoon cooking oil in a large saucepan over a medium-high heat. Add the lamb pieces and sear them until they are browned on all sides (don't overcrowd the pan; you may need to do this in batches). Add the garlic, spices, 1/2 teaspoon salt and 1/4 teaspoon pepper and gently fry for a few minutes before adding enough hot water to just cover the meat. Bring to a simmer and cook, uncovered, for 5 minutes, removing any scum that comes to the surface with a spoon. Reduce the heat, cover and cook for about 1 1/4 hours, or until the meat is tender. After 1 hour, rinse the rice in cold water until the water runs clear, then put it to soak in a large bowl of water for 15 minutes.

When the lamb is cooked, whisk together the *kashk*, yogurt and egg along with half a mug of hot cooking broth from the pot. Slowly add this to the lamb, a little at a time, stirring as you pour. It's important to add this mixture in stages so that it doesn't curdle. Add the chickpeas, cover and cook for about 10 minutes, keeping it at a gentle simmer over a low heat, then take the lid off and cook for another 10 minutes, so that the sauce thickens around the meat. Taste and adjust the seasoning if necessary.

Meanwhile, begin to cook the rice. Crush the saffron with the sugar in a mortar and pestle, then add 2 tablespoons of just-boiled water. Drain the rice. Melt the butter in a saucepan. Add the rice to the pan with 2½ cups/600ml just-boiled water, the saffron liquid, cardamom and 1 teaspoon salt. Stir well and bring to the boil, then reduce the heat, cover the rice with a few paper towels, then the lid and cook for 10 minutes. Remove from the heat and leave the rice to rest for 5 minutes.

Preheat the oven to 400°F/200°C. Toss the bread pieces in a couple of tablespoons of cooking oil and place them in the oven to crisp up for 7–10 minutes.

Toast the pine nuts by dry-frying them in a small pan over a medium heat for a minute or so, until they turn golden brown.

To serve, transfer the rice to a large serving platter and spoon over the lamb and chickpeas. Top with the toasted pieces of bread and finish with a sprinkle of pine nuts, the parsley and a couple of teaspoons of sumac.

Pictured on page 184

# Slow-roast shoulder of lamb with Palestinian spices

This show-stopping roast is a great dish for entertaining. When slow-roasted in this way, the lamb becomes so meltingly soft that it falls off the bone, perfect for stuffing into pockets of flatbread alongside salads, yogurt and pickles, shawarma-style. Start it the night before, so the marinade has a chance to infuse the lamb. The pomegranate molasses will blacken a little in the oven, but don't worry, that isn't a sign that the meat is burning, it will still be utterly juicy and succulent under the crust.

**Serves 6**

4½ lb./2kg whole shoulder of lamb, on the bone
3 tablespoons extra virgin olive oil
about ½ cup/100ml unsweetened pomegranate molasses
5 garlic cloves, crushed
½ cup/25g cilantro, leaves and stalks, finely chopped, plus more to serve
1½ tablespoons dried mint
1½ teaspoons ground cumin
1½ teaspoons ground allspice
1½ tablespoons sumac, plus more to serve
sea salt and freshly ground black pepper
handful of pomegranate seeds, to serve

The day before you want to eat, place the lamb in a large roasting dish and slash the meat in a cross-hatch fashion on both sides, cutting deeply and right down to the bone.

Mix the remaining ingredients together, except the pomegranate seeds, seasoning with 2½ teaspoons salt and 1 teaspoon pepper. Rub this marinade into the meat, then spend some time massaging it into all the little nooks and crannies. Cover and place in the fridge to marinate overnight.

The next day, take the lamb out of the fridge 20 minutes before you cook it so it comes to room temperature. Preheat the oven to 325°F/160°C.

Pour a mug of just-boiled water into the roasting dish, then place the lamb in the middle of the oven. After 30 minutes, cover it with foil to stop the edges burning and baste the meat every hour. Cook for about 4 hours. You'll know it is ready when it is so soft that you can easily pull the meat from the bone.

When the lamb is cooked, leave it to rest for 15 minutes. Scatter with pomegranate seeds and cilantro just before serving, and have some sumac handy at the table to sprinkle over each portion.

# Stuffed zucchini
# with spiced beef or lamb

KOUSA MAHSHI

This dish takes inspiration from an afternoon I spent cooking with Safa Tamish in Akka. Safa showed me how to make *sheikh el mahshi*— the king of Palestinian stuffed vegetables—and we spent a hilarious afternoon giggling like schoolchildren at my failed attempts to stuff zucchini the size of my finger. In short, I made a total hash of it, clearly not having fingers as nimble and dextrous as hers, so I hope she won't mind that I changed the recipe to make it a bit more clumsy-person-friendly, using larger zucchini and swapping the yogurt for tahini, but still keeping a meaty, flavorsome stuffing that is worthy of a sheikh.

**Serves 4**

FOR THE STUFFED ZUCCHINI
4 large zucchini
olive oil or any neutral oil
sea salt and freshly ground
   black pepper
3 garlic cloves, crushed
8 oz./250g ground beef or
   lamb
2 tablespoons unsweetened
   pomegranate molasses
1/2 teaspoon ground allspice
1/2 teaspoon ground cumin
1/2 teaspoon ground cinnamon
1/2 teaspoon ground turmeric
pinch of cayenne pepper
handful of chopped
   parsley leaves

FOR THE SAUCE
3 tablespoons tahini
3 tablespoons lemon juice,
   or more to taste
1/2 garlic clove, crushed

Preheat the oven to 400°F/200°C.

Slice the zucchini in half and scoop out their insides with a teaspoon, reserving them, leaving hollow vegetables with a shell about 1/4 in./5mm thick. Place the hollowed-out zucchini on a baking sheet, drizzle with cooking oil and sprinkle with 1/2 teaspoon salt.

Finely chop the zucchini flesh you scooped out and place it on another baking sheet, drizzling with cooking oil and 1/4 teaspoon salt.

Transfer both sheets to the oven and cook for around 30 minutes until the zucchini have softened. Don't worry if they have charred a little bit, as this will impart a nice smoky flavor. The chopped zucchini won't take that long, so check on it after 15 minutes and remove it from the oven when it's ready.

Meanwhile, make the meat stuffing. Heat 1 tablespoon cooking oil in a pan over a medium heat and add the crushed garlic. Fry for a few minutes, then add the ground meat. Fry the meat until it has browned all over, then add the pomegranate molasses and spices, 3/4 teaspoon salt and 1/2 teaspoon pepper. Pour in 7 tablespoons/ 100ml hot water, cover and cook over a low heat for 30 minutes. Depending on the quality of your meat, it might take a little longer to soften, so taste and adjust both the seasoning and the cooking time accordingly.

Make the topping by combining the roasted zucchini flesh with the tahini, lemon juice and garlic. Taste and adjust the seasoning with salt and pepper, or more lemon juice, if you want.

When the hollow zucchini halves have cooked, remove from the oven and stuff with the meat. Top with the thick zucchini and tahini sauce and finish with a sprinkling of parsley.

# Lamb meatballs with tahini

KEFTE BI TAHINI

There are dozens of different types of *kefte* (meatballs) eaten in the Palestinian kitchen, but of all of them this is my firm favorite. The unique combination of sticky roasted potatoes, spicy ground lamb and garlicky tahini never fails to delight. You can prepare the potatoes, meatballs and tahini sauce all in advance, then just assemble the dish and pop it into the oven about 30 minutes before you want to eat. I recommend going to a butcher and asking for some ground shoulder of lamb for this dish, as I think it has the best flavor, and you can also get them to trim off any excess fat before grinding the meat. Use a large ovenproof dish that doubles up as a serving platter for this recipe, so you can take the finished dish straight to the table.

**Serves 6 as part of a spread, or 4 as a stand-alone dish**

FOR THE POTATOES
1½ lb./700g potatoes
sea salt
2 tablespoons olive oil or any neutral oil

FOR THE KEFTE
1¾ lb./800g ground lamb
1 onion, finely chopped
⅓ cup/25g parsley leaves, roughly chopped
3 garlic cloves, crushed
½ teaspoon chilli flakes
1½ teaspoons ground cinnamon
1½ teaspoons ground allspice
freshly ground black pepper
2 tablespoons extra virgin olive oil

FOR THE TAHINI SAUCE
3 teaspoons/75g tahini
2 tablespoons lemon juice, plus more to taste
1 garlic clove, crushed
¼ cup/10g chopped parsley leaves, plus more to serve

FOR THE TOPPING
¼ cup/30g pine nuts
1 tablespoon/15g salted butter

Preheat the oven to 350°F/180°C. Peel the potatoes and then slice them into ¼ in./1cm-thick discs. Place them in a large ovenproof dish in a single layer, sprinkle over ½ teaspoon salt and the cooking oil and toss to evenly coat. Bake for around 40 minutes, or until they are soft.

Meanwhile, make the *kefte* by placing all the ingredients, except the extra virgin olive oil, in a food processor, seasoning with 1 teaspoon salt and ½ teaspoon pepper. Blitz for a few minutes to evenly combine. (Grinding the meat twice in this way also ensures a better texture.) Mold the meatballs into 2 in./5cm oval shapes. Put the extra virgin olive oil in a bowl and, using your fingertips, lightly coat each ball with oil to smooth it. (At this stage you can leave the *kefte* for a few hours in the fridge if you are preparing the meal ahead of time.)

Continued on page 194

When the potatoes are soft, place the *kefte* in a layer on top of them and bake for 15–20 minutes, until just cooked through.

Make the tahini sauce by whisking all the ingredients together, seasoning with 1/2 teaspoon salt and adding 1/4 cup/75ml water. As varieties of tahini can vary, add a bit more water or lemon juice
if it seems a little thick; you want the consistency of runny honey.

For the topping, fry the pine nuts in the butter until they are golden, then place on a paper towel to soak up excess oil.

Once the lamb is cooked, drain off any excess fat that has been released during cooking, then spoon over the tahini sauce and top with the pine nuts and chopped parsley.

Serve immediately.

# Pan-baked lamb kibbeh

KIBBEH BIL SANEEYEH

*Kibbeh* is the prized feasting dish of Palestinian food, with dozens of different variations across the region. This baked version is somewhat akin to a meat pie and makes for a hearty and filling main course, best served with a simple, crunchy Everyday Palestinian salad (see page 81). You'll need an ovenproof dish around 12 x 10 in./30 x 25cm that can double up as a serving dish.

Serves 4–6

FOR THE CRUST
1¾ cups/250g fine bulgur wheat
3½ oz./100g ground lamb
1 onion, roughly chopped
1 teaspoon ground cinnamon
1 teaspoon ground cumin
1 teaspoon dried oregano
chopped parsley leaves, to serve

FOR THE FILLING
3 tablespoons olive oil or any neutral oil
1 onion, finely chopped
½ teaspoon cumin seeds
½ teaspoon coriander seeds
½ teaspoon ground cinnamon
½ teaspoon ground allspice
3 garlic cloves, crushed
1¼ lb./600g ground lamb
2 tablespoons unsweetened pomegranate molasses
sea salt and freshly ground black pepper
about ½ cup/60g pine nuts

FOR THE YOGURT AND CUCUMBER SAUCE
7 oz./200g cucumber (any type)
2 cups/500g unflavored yogurt
½ garlic clove, crushed
small handful of fresh mint leaves, finely chopped
1 teaspoon dried mint

Place the bulgur wheat in a large bowl and pour over enough just-boiled water to cover it by 2 in./5cm. Set aside and leave to soak for 30 minutes.

To make the filling, heat 2 tablespoons of the cooking oil in a large pan, add the onion and fry over a medium heat for about 10 minutes until softened.

Toast the cumin and coriander seeds in a dry frying pan for a few minutes until their aromas have been released, then crush in a mortar and pestle or a spice grinder. Add these spices to the onion along with the cinnamon, allspice and garlic and fry for a few minutes before adding the lamb, pomegranate molasses, 1 teaspoon salt and ½ teaspoon pepper. Cook over a medium-high heat for a few minutes to brown the meat, then cover, reduce the heat and cook for 15 minutes, stirring occasionally.

Continued on page 197 and pictured on next page

Meanwhile, place all the crust ingredients, except the bulgur wheat and parsley, in a food processor with 1 teaspoon salt and 1/2 teaspoon pepper. Blend until you have a smooth paste. Tip this mixture into a large bowl and add the bulgur wheat, which by now should have soaked up all the water. Use your hands to mix it all together.

Fry the pine nuts for the filling in the remaining 1 tablespoon cooking oil in a small pan for a minute or so until golden brown, then tip onto a paper towel to remove excess oil.

Preheat the oven to 400°F/200°C.

Now you can assemble the *kibbeh*. Using your hands, press half the crust mixture into the base of a 12 x 10 in./30 x 25cm ovenproof serving dish. Top with the cooked lamb and pine nuts, then finish with the remaining crust mixture. For this top layer, I find it most effective to make little patties with my hands, then place them on top of the meat, squishing them together so there are no gaps. Smooth the *kibbeh* crust with the back of a spoon (you may want to use a little cold water to assist with this), then score the surface diagonally in a cross-hatch fashion with a knife.

Bake for 50–60 minutes, or until the *kibbeh* crust is dark brown and crunchy.

Meanwhile, make the yogurt sauce. Cut the cucumber in half and, using a teaspoon, scoop out and discard all its seeds. Chop the flesh into small cubes and mix them into the yogurt with the garlic, fresh and dried mint and 1/4 teaspoon salt.

When the kibbeh is browned, take it out of the oven and leave it to rest for 10 minutes.

When you are ready to eat, scatter it with a handful of chopped parsley and serve with the yogurt sauce and a salad.

# Bethlehem

The air felt crisp against my face as I wandered into the fruit tree-filled garden of my guest house in Bethlehem. I took a seat on a swinging bench that was nestled under a canopy of vine leaves, pulling my woollen scarf tighter around my neck to shield me from the cold as I listened to the soaring vocals of the early evening *adhaan* (the Muslim call to prayer) echoing across the sky.

I was soon joined by Zarouk, the owner of the guest house, who greeted me with a cup of tea he told me is brewed from the extracts of 20 plants he grows in his garden. I sipped the aromatic concoction and started guessing its ingredients. "There's sage," I began, "and mint, lemon, za'atar and ginger." The others came slower as I rolled the warm, heady herbal tea around my mouth: a hint of marjoram, maybe some bay leaf, orange zest for sure. It was warming, soothing and comforting, and I poured myself another cup.

Zarouk's family have lived in the guest house for several generations. It used to be their family home, but now serves as a welcome base for tourists from around the world who flock to Bethlehem to visit the Church of the Nativity and Manger Square, where Jesus is said to have been born. I was there on a very different pilgrimage: to find the town's best hummus and falafel. Zarouk told me to head to Afteem's in the center of the city ("It's where President Obama ate when he came here!") so my photographer Raya and I walked there for breakfast.

Arriving at the café at 8am, we saw tables already filled with of groups of Palestinian men eating. On the steps outside, we passed a metal deep-fryer where balls of falafel were dropped into sizzling hot oil, crackling and sputtering until golden and crisp, ready to be stuffed into pockets of flatbread and smothered with hummus. We took a seat in the cavernous stone interior and waited for our presidential breakfasts, stomachs rumbling in anticipation.

They did not disappoint. The hummus was whipped silky-smooth and light as air, pleasingly laden with nutty tahini. Mine arrived with *musabaha* topping, a glistening heap of lemony chickpeas adorning the purée, and finished with a thick slick of extra virgin olive oil. Chunky slices of tomatoes, onions, brined cucumber pickles and hot green chillies arrived, as well as a fiery red pepper sauce into which we tentatively dipped our crunchy falafel. My mouth was awakened by intense astringency and chilli heat, as smooth hummus and crunchy falafel provided a riot of textures and flavors.

—

After breakfast, we wandered through the markets of Bethlehem, passing shop after shop selling tourist handicrafts and religious memorabilia. After paying our respects at the Church of the Nativity, we made our way to one of Bethlehem's more infamous sites, the Separation Wall, to admire some of British graffiti artist Banksy's stencils.

Images and slogans cover vast sections of the concrete and steel wall and we followed its winding route through to Aida refugee camp, one of the oldest camps in the OPT, home to Palestinian refugees from Jerusalem and the villages west of Hebron, who were forcibly displaced when the state of Israel was created in 1948. We were here to visit Alrowwad, a creative arts community group that runs theater and dance performances in the camp, and also puts on cooking classes for foreign visitors to learn traditional Palestinian recipes from the refugees. I was given a tour by Manal Odeh, who grew up in the camp and now helps organize the cooking classes. "We teach how to make traditional dishes like *maqloubeh* and *maftool*," she told me. "It's a great way for people to talk and share with each other."

Manal took us on a walking tour of the densely populated camp, talking us through her favorite recipes and giving us a rundown of the ingredients for which Bethlehem is renowned. Just as we finished talking about the area's bountiful vegetables, Manal's husband pulled up in his car, his trunk crammed with freshly harvested cauliflowers the size of my forearm. Raya and I stared, dumbfounded, never having seen cauliflowers of that size before, and Manal laughed, telling us her best way of preparing them: fried with warming allspice and cumin, then drizzled with tahini. My mouth watered at the thought and I promised to cook it as soon as I got home.

—

Coming from a family of farmers, I've always been fascinated by seed preservation, so I was excited to move on to speak to Vivien Sansour, a pioneering agriculturalist and botanist from the neighboring village of Beit Sahour. Vivien is a founder of The Palestine Seed Library, set up to preserve heirloom Palestinian seeds. She works with farmers, teachers and students, writing down seed stories, collecting the oral history of the land.

"I lived outside Palestine for many years," Vivien tells me. "And when I came home I saw that our food had changed. Instead of selling local produce, the markets were drenched with 'agribusiness' goods. I was looking for the vegetables I ate when I was younger and I found they were gone. We loved purple carrots and I missed how my mother would cook them in carob sauce. All of a sudden, they were not available. Looking for a purple carrot was a bit like searching for illegal drugs! So I decided to do something about it."

Vivien studies and grows varieties of seeds that are at risk of extinction and encourages farmers to use them instead of hybrid seeds bought each year from corporations.

"The aim of my project is to save Palestinian seeds, record their story and cultural significance and propagate them, so people here can learn more about their agricultural heritage. A big part of this is also putting energy into keeping our soil the best quality that it can be, away from harsh chemicals."

Vivien has a mobile kitchen that she drives around villages to re-introduce farmers to cooking with ingredients that grow wild around the West Bank. "What is so tragic for me about the Israeli settlements is that, yes, they are being built on top of our land, but also they are being built on top of our food. We are a traditional agrarian community and have such an intimate relationship with these mountains; eating foraged foods is a huge part of Palestinian culinary heritage. When I see where the Wall is being built now and how it is destroying our beautiful fields of wild asparagus, it breaks my heart."

—

Heading south to the village of Ayub, we visited the garden farm of Rania Abed and her family, a small plot of land where she grows eggplants, tomatoes, pumpkins and zucchini as well as all manner of fragrant herbs, and fruit such as peaches, grapes, figs, lemons, oranges, cactus, prickly pears and pomegranates. "This is part of our survival," Rania told me as we wandered through her garden looking for eggplants to harvest for lunch. "We must depend on the land, in case anything happens. If you have olive oil, tomatoes, bread and za'atar, you can survive."

Rania told me how she preserves seasonal produce: making jams, conserves and pickles and drying fruit. "This is Palestinian food and culture," she said. "Preserving whatever you have and then distributing it around your family. My sister-in-law has lots of cucumbers

and zucchini in the summer and we have beans, peas and cauliflowers, so we simply exchange. Sharing is how our communities survive." We gathered the vegetables we needed and returned to the kitchen, where Rania set me to work stuffing eggplants and peppers with lamb and rice.

Rania was born in the Old City in Jerusalem, but moved to this village, south of Bethlehem, after she got married. "I loved the time I spent in Al Aqsa mosque when I was little," she told me. "Around the mosque there is a courtyard and trees and space and we spent almost all our childhood there." Her culinary knowledge isn't strictly Jerusalemite through. "My grandmother is from Haifa and my mum is from Gaza so we had both those influences in our kitchen. But in Jerusalem we cook dishes with pumpkin and lots of fried onions and tamarind, a combination of sweet and sour that is so delicious!" She brought her thumb and forefingers together and kissed them, smacking her lips in delight.

—

Cooking is thirsty work, so we took a break from the kitchen to visit Palestine's first micro-brewery. Taybeh is a family-owned business established in 1994 when two brothers, David and Nadim Khoury—driven by a passion for Palestine and a love of lager— came up with the idea to establish a Palestinian beer company. Their goal was to produce natural, hand-crafted beers with no preservatives or additives, that not only

tasted fantastic but would also help to boost the Palestinian economy. Nadim turned his hobby of making home-made beer during his university days into professional expertise and is now the master brewer of the company. We met him and his daughter Madees at their factory, in the hills of Taybeh, a village in the West Bank. They welcomed us with a selection of their golden, amber, dark and white beers. The golden beer was crisp and refreshing, the amber earthy and smooth, the dark beer tasted like autumn... but the white beer captivated me the most, with its hints of cilantro and orange zest.

"The spices are from Jericho," Nadim told me proudly. "Our beers have the natural flavors of Palestine." Producing as organic a product as possible is an important part of the company's ethos. "We make the beer with a 21-day ferment, without adding anything to speed up the process," said Madees, as she topped up our glasses with the cold ale.

The brewery exports to Japan, Denmark, Sweden, the UK, Spain, Italy and the US. "Being sold in Germany and Denmark is an honor for us," Nadim told us, "as they have thousands of their own high-quality beers."

Taking inspiration from their German partners, the Taybeh factory also hosts an annual "Oktoberfest" which attracts around 15,000 visitors. "It is an opportunity to get away from all the craziness and celebrate the good things Palestine has to offer," Madees said. "You get Israelis, Palestinians, Muslims, Christians from here, but also lots of

internationals. The festival brings people together and shows a different side of Palestine to that which foreigners expect."

Madees studied brewing in China and Germany and, for her, working for the family business has a higher significance than just producing beer. "What we see on the news is so different to what Palestine is like in real life. When people think of Palestinians, they just see fighting, but there is another side to us. We have fun, we listen to music, we dance, we drink beer. We want to show the world that we are normal, we want to show a new face of Palestine."

But running a microbrewery in the OPT has not been easy. "We have faced so many obstacles, you could write a book just about that!" Nadim laughed. "The check points, the sieges, the closures, the changing of the borders all affects us. You can never be certain what will happen when you go through a check point. Our product is a natural beer, so it cannot resist the heat of the sun for six or seven hours if we are held, and sometimes a whole batch can get spoiled."

But this doesn't deter the Khoury family. "When I think about how we can create a viable Palestinian state, one part of that is to depend on our own economy instead of being reliant on international aid. We need a sustainable local economy and producing our own beer is part of that." He cracked open another bottle for us to share, warming to his theme. "We might be under occupation but one day we will get our freedom... and when we do, we'll celebrate with a beer!"

# DESSERTS

From sticky syrup-drenched pastries flavored with rose water and cardamom, to warm, sweet cheese-filled pies and coconut-speckled cakes, the Palestinian kitchen embraces delectable treats to suit every taste.

In common with most countries in the Middle East, Palestinians don't traditionally eat a dessert to end meals. Instead, sweets are enjoyed throughout the day with cups of tea and coffee. This suits me just fine, as I adore sweet baked goods and just as happily eat them for breakfast as after dinner. Every Palestinian neighborhood has a few bakeries or patisseries, serving up an assortment of cookies, cakes, baklava, *knafeh* and biscuits, and the flavors I've encountered in those local haunts inspired all the recipes in this chapter.

# Pomegranate passion cake

Pomegranates never fail to delight me; their crimson juices and sweet and tart arils provided such joy for me throughout my childhood that they are forever etched in my memory and on my heart. Palestinians also hold this mighty fruit in high esteem, and here I've paired it with a dense and sticky almond cake, topped with a light and creamy mascarpone topping, which I love, and which I hope will enliven your passion for this magical fruit, too. You will need an 8 in./20 cm cake pan.

**Serves 8**

### FOR THE CAKE
1¾ sticks/200g unsalted butter, plus more for the pan
¾ cup/170g superfine sugar
4 eggs, lightly beaten
¾ cup/100g flour
¼ teaspoon fine sea salt
1½ teaspoons baking powder
about 3 cups/270g ground almonds
finely grated zest of 1 unwaxed lemon
3 tablespoons lemon juice
2 tablespoons unsweetened pomegranate molasses
1 teaspoon vanilla extract

### FOR THE GLAZE
3 tablespoons unsweetened pomegranate molasses
2 tablespoons sugar

### FOR THE TOPPING
1 cup/150g pomegranate seeds
2 tablespoons superfine sugar
1 cup/250g mascarpone
3 tablespoons Greek yogurt
1 tablespoon confectioner's sugar

Preheat the oven to 325°F/160°C. Butter an 8 in./20cm cake pan and line it with parchment paper.

In a large bowl, cream the butter and sugar with an electric mixer. When the mixture is combined, beat in the eggs gradually, beating well between each addition. Then fold in the flour, salt, baking powder and almonds with a large spoon. Fold in the lemon zest and juice, pomegranate molasses and vanilla, then spoon into the prepared pan. Bake for about 45-50 minutes, or until firm and a skewer inserted into the center comes out clean.

When it is almost ready, make the glaze. Put the pomegranate molasses and sugar in a saucepan with 3 tablespoons water, place over a medium heat and stir to help the sugar dissolve. As soon as the cake comes out of the oven, use a fork to pierce holes in it, then brush the syrup over. Leave to cool in the pan, then turn it out, syrup-side up.

Place the pomegranate seeds in a small bowl with the sugar and leave to macerate for at least 30 minutes. Mix the mascarpone with the yogurt and confectioner's sugar and spread it thickly over the cake. Finish with the pomegranate seeds and their juices.

# Spiced pumpkin, olive oil and orange cake

This is a cake you can turn to when you need to lift your mood as, while it bakes, it fills the kitchen with the uplifting scent of sweet pumpkin married with the warming fragrances of cinnamon, ginger and cloves. It is a dense and supremely moist cake, using olive oil instead of butter for a wonderfully soft, tender crumb. I use canned pumpkin for this recipe but, if you want to make pumpkin purée yourself, roast around 14 oz./400g peeled, deseeded and chopped pumpkin for about 30 minutes or until completely soft. After it has cooled, push it through a sieve to get rid of excess liquid. The cake keeps well in an airtight container for a couple of days. You'll need a 10 x 4 in./25 x 13cm loaf pan.

Serves 6-8

FOR THE CAKE
2/3 cup/150ml olive oil or any neutral oil, plus more for the pan
1 cup/200g superfine sugar
1/4 cup/50ml extra virgin olive oil
finely grated zest of 1/2 organic or unwaxed orange
3 eggs
1 1/2 cups/200g flour
1 1/2 teaspoons baking powder
1/2 teaspoon baking soda
1/2 teaspoon ground cinnamon
1/2 teaspoon ground allspice
1/2 teaspoon ground ginger
pinch of ground cloves
1/4 teaspoon sea salt
1 cup/250g cooked pumpkin purée, canned or home-made (see recipe introduction)
1 teaspoon lemon juice

FOR THE ICING
2 cups/250g confectioner's sugar
finely grated zest of 1/2 organic or unwaxed orange
2-3 tablespoons orange juice
1 teaspoon lemon juice
unsalted pistachio nibs, to serve

Preheat the oven to 350°F/180°C. Lightly oil a 10 x 4 in./ 25 x 13cm loaf pan and line it with parchment paper. With an electric mixer, beat the sugar, both oils and the orange zest until combined and smooth. Gradually beat in the eggs, one by one, until the batter turns paler. Sift all the dry ingredients and gently stir them in. Finally, fold in the pumpkin purée and lemon juice, being careful not to lose too much air from the mixture.

Pour the batter into the prepared pan and bake in the center of the oven for around 50 minutes, or until a skewer inserted into the cake comes out clean. Remove from the oven, leave to cool in the pan for 10 minutes, then tip it out onto a wire rack.

When the cake is completely cool, make the icing. Mix the confectioner's sugar with the orange zest, 2 tablespoons of orange juice and the lemon juice until you have a thick paste. If you need to loosen it a bit, add 1 teaspoon more orange juice at a time. Spoon the icing over the cake and finish with a sprinkling of pistachio nibs.

# Chocolate and coconut cake

There's a delightful Palestinian restaurant in Haifa called Douzan, run by Fadi Najir, an exuberant and charming man (see page 69). On one of my visits there, I ate the most delectable chocolate and coconut cake, it was moist, dense and sticky all at once. I have no idea what Fadi's recipe is, but this is my ode to that sweet experience, with the addition of a thick, luxurious chocolate ganache topping for good measure. You will need an 8 inch/20 cm cake pan.

**Serves 8**

FOR THE CAKE
1 ¾ sticks/200g unsalted butter, plus more for the pan
1 cup/200g superfine sugar
3 eggs
1½ cups/200g all-purpose flour
¾ cup/65g cocoa powder
1½ teaspoons baking powder
¼ teaspoon fine sea salt
1¼ cups/100g shredded coconut, plus more to decorate
¾ cup/185ml whole milk
1 teaspoon vanilla extract

FOR THE GANACHE
1 cup/284ml heavy cream
8 oz./250g good-quality dark chocolate, roughly chopped
3 tablespoons confectioner's sugar (optional)

Preheat the oven to 350°F/180°C. Butter an 8 in./20 cm cake pan and line the base with parchment paper.

Place the butter and sugar in a bowl of an electric mixer fitted with the whisk attachment and beat until light and creamy. Beat in the eggs, one by one, then sift in the flour, cocoa, baking powder and salt and fold through with the coconut, using a large spoon. Finally, stir in the milk and vanilla extract.

Pour the cake batter into the pan and transfer to the oven. Bake for around 35 minutes, or until a skewer inserted into the cake comes out clean.

Leave the cake in the pan for 5 minutes, then transfer to a wire rack to completely cool.

To make the ganache, pour the cream into a saucepan and bring to the boil. Remove from the heat and add the dark chocolate. Stir until all the chocolate has fully melted. Let the mixture cool to room temperature, then whip it using the electric mixer for a few minutes until it is fluffy and has lightened in color. Taste and add the confectioner's sugar, if you want it sweeter. Spoon this over the cake and finish with a smattering of shredded coconut.

# Apricot and rose water
# rice pudding

ROZ BIL HALIB

This rich and soothing pudding is the dessert equivalent of a big warm hug. As varieties of rose water vary in strength, I recommend adding it in stages then tasting and increasing the amount to your preference. Any leftovers make for a rather wonderful, mood-enhancing breakfast.

Serves 4

FOR THE RICE PUDDING
4 cups/1 liter whole milk (or unsweetened soy milk or coconut milk)
1/3 cup/75g sugar
1 teaspoon vanilla extract
seeds from 8 cardamom pods, crushed
about 1 cup/160g pudding rice, or other short-grain rice
fine sea salt
1 1/2 tablespoons rose water

FOR THE APRICOT COMPOTE
4 1/2 oz./125g dried apricots, roughly chopped
2 teaspoons lemon juice
seeds from 2 cardamom pods, crushed
2 tablespoons honey
1 teaspoon rose water

OPTIONAL TOPPINGS
2 tablespoons unsalted pistachio nibs, chopped
1 tablespoon edible dried rose petals

Place the milk, sugar, vanilla extract and crushed cardamom seeds in a large saucepan and bring to the boil, stirring occasionally until the sugar has dissolved. Add the rice and a generous pinch of salt, cover and simmer for 30–40 minutes, or until the rice is cooked and very soft. Give the pot a stir every few minutes so the rice doesn't stick and, if it looks a bit dry, add 1/2 cup/150ml just-boiled water to loosen it.

Meanwhile, make the compote. Place the apricots, lemon juice and cardamom in a small saucepan over a medium heat and pour in 3/4 cup/200ml just-boiled water. Bring to a simmer, then cover and let the apricots cook for around 10 minutes. Add the honey, cooking for a further 5–10 minutes, or until the apricots are soft. Add the rose water gradually to taste and take off the heat.

When the rice is cooked, stir in the rose water—again gradually, to taste—and cook for a final few minutes.

To serve, spoon into glasses and top with the compote. If you like, scatter with chopped pistachio nibs and rose petals.

# Mtabaq

These sweet and sticky cheese-filled parcels are my dessert of choice whenever I am in Jerusalem. The word *mtabaq* means 'folded' in Arabic and, here, thin sheets of buttery filo pastry are folded over melted cheese, then doused with cardamom-infused syrup. These are best eaten as soon as they're made, but you can assemble the parcels slightly ahead of time and then just pop them in the oven 30 minutes before you are planning to serve them. Traditionally, *akkawi* cheese is used to make this and you'll be able to find that in Middle Eastern stores. Alternatively, I use a mix of ricotta and mozzarella, which is more readily available.

**Makes 6**

**FOR THE MTABAQ**
6 tablespoons/90g salted butter, melted
36 sheets of filo pastry, each 8 in./20cm square
1½ lb./750g grated *akkawi* cheese, or 1 lb./500g ricotta mixed with 8 oz./250g grated mozzarella
crushed unsalted pistachios, to serve

**FOR THE SYRUP**
1⅓ cup/260g superfine sugar
seeds from 3 cardamom pods, crushed
1 tablespoon lemon juice

Brush the base of a large baking pan with melted butter. Place a sheet of filo pastry in the pan and brush it with melted butter. Layer 5 more sheets on top, brushing each with butter as you go. (Keep the remaining filo covered with a clean, damp dish towel while you work, to prevent it drying out.)

Divide the cheese into 6 portions. Spoon 1 portion into the middle of the pastry and use your fingers to spread it in a square, leaving a 2 in./5cm frame around it.

Fold 1 corner of the pastry layers into the middle and repeat for the remaining corners until you have a square parcel. Turn seam side down, brush with a little more butter, then use a sharp knife to cut through the top layers in a cross shape. Repeat to fill and shape 6 pastries. At this stage, you could leave the *m'tabaq* for up to 1 hour, but not much longer, or the filo can become soggy.

Preheat the oven to 450°F/230°C. Bake the parcels for 15–20 minutes, or until crisp and golden brown.

Halfway through cooking, make the syrup. Pour ½ cup/120ml water into a saucepan and place over a medium heat, adding the sugar and cardamom. Bring to the boil, stirring to help the sugar dissolve, then add the lemon juice and simmer for 2 minutes.

As soon as you take the pastries out of the oven, pour the hot syrup evenly over (3–4 tablespoons on each should do it). Leave for 5 minutes, then sprinkle with crushed pistachios and serve.

# Fig and almond tart

The fig is one of the most emblematic fruits of ancient Palestine and, in Arab mythology, represents abundance in all its forms. During my travels, I visited the village of Majd al-Krum in northern Galilee, which is famed for its figs. I spent an afternoon walking through its fertile orchards, under tall trees heavily laden with these dark purple and juicy fruits, and was inspired to create a recipe that brought them together with almonds, one of the land's other primary crops. As it can be somewhat challenging to source truly sweet figs unless you live in a Mediterranean climate, I recommend baking the fruit in a little honey first, as I do here, to give them a good start. Use a fluted 9 in./23cm diameter tart pan to make this, and serve with heavy cream or vanilla ice cream on the side. If you like the floral notes of orange blossom water, a teaspoon added to the filling would work very well, too.

Serves 8

### FOR THE PASTRY

1¾ cups/220g all-purpose flour, sifted, plus more to dust
⅓ cup/40g confectioner's sugar
¼ teaspoon fine sea salt
1 stick/120g unsalted butter, cut into small cubes
finely grated zest of ½ organic or unwaxed orange
1 egg yolk
2–4 tablespoons cold water

### FOR THE FILLING

8 ripe figs
3 tablespoons honey
1¾ sticks/200g unsalted butter
¾ cup plus 2 tablespoons/175g superfine sugar
2 cups/200g ground almonds
finely grated zest of ½ organic or unwaxed orange
2 eggs, lightly beaten
1 teaspoon vanilla extract
¼ teaspoon fine sea salt
1 teaspoon orange blossom water (optional)

Start with the pastry. Place the flour, sugar and salt in a large bowl and use your hands to rub in the butter until you have a texture resembling crumbs. (You can also do this in an electric mixer fitted with a paddle attachment, mixing on a slow speed.)

Add the zest and egg yolk, then slowly add the water 1 tablespoon at a time, mixing constantly, until you have a smooth dough. You might not need all the water, so add it in stages. Be careful not to work the dough too much, as it can make the pastry chewy and elastic instead of crumbly and short.

Mold the dough into a ball, cover with plastic wrap and leave it to rest in the fridge for at least 1 hour.

When you are ready to bake the tart, preheat the oven to 350°F/180°C. Take the pastry out of the fridge and let it come to room temperature while you prepare the figs.

Cut the stems off each fruit then slice the figs in half lengthways. Place them on a baking sheet cut side up, drizzle over the honey and roast in the oven for 10 minutes.

Continued on next page

Leave the oven on as you roll out your pastry. Lightly flour a work top and rolling pin, then roll the pastry out to about ¼ in./5mm thick.

Line the base and sides of a 9 in./23cm diameter fluted tart pan with the pastry, pushing it into the crevices so you get an even layer. Prick the base of the pastry a few times with a fork, then line it with parchment paper and fill it with baking beans or other dried beans.

Bake the tart crust for 15 minutes, then remove the paper and beans and bake for a further 5–10 minutes, until the pastry looks golden. Take the pastry out of the oven and let it cool slightly while you make the filling.

Cream the butter and sugar in an electric mixer or by hand with a wooden spoon until it is smooth and pale. Add the ground almonds, orange zest, eggs, vanilla and salt. (If you want to add orange blossom water, do so now.) Spoon the mixture on top of the pastry. Press the figs into the almond mixture; the honey will all have been absorbed by the fruit.

Transfer the tart to the oven and bake for 45 minutes, or until golden all over. Leave it in the pan for 10 minutes, then transfer to a wire rack to cool.

# Spiced Medjool sticky pudding

Rich, indulgent, sticky in all the right places, this pudding is a celebration of the Palestinian Medjool date. With a thick caramel sauce that highlights the dense, buttery sweetness of these dates, it is a hefty dessert for when you are in need of some serious comforting. I like to serve it with a scoop of vanilla ice cream and follow it with a nice lie-down on the sofa. Use a 8 in./20cm square baking dish.

**Serves 6**

FOR THE PUDDING
6 oz./180g Medjool dates, pitted and finely chopped
1 teaspoon baking soda
6 tablespoons/85g unsalted butter, softened
½ cup plus 1 tablespoon/ 100g dark brown sugar
2 eggs
3 tablespoons/60ml whole milk
1 teaspoon vanilla extract
1¼ cups/175g all-purpose flour, sifted
1 teaspoon baking powder
¾ teaspoon ground allspice
¾ teaspoon ground cinnamon
5 cloves, ground
¼ teaspoon fine sea salt
½ cup/50g walnuts, roughly chopped

FOR THE SAUCE
½ cup/250ml heavy cream
6 tablespoons/85g unsalted butter
½ cup/85g dark brown sugar
pinch of fine sea salt

Preheat the oven to 350°F/180°C.

Place the dates and bicarb in a saucepan with 1 cup/250ml just-boiled water. Simmer over a medium heat for 4 minutes, switch off the heat and leave to soak for 10 minutes, then roughly mash with a fork.

Cream the butter and sugar together with an electric mixer until paler. Beat in the eggs, one by one, beating well after each addition, then add the milk and vanilla extract and beat again.

Fold in the flour, baking powder, spices and salt with a large spoon, then finally fold in the mashed dates and the walnuts. Spoon into an 8 in./20cm square baking dish and cook in the oven for about 35 minutes. It should be firm on top, but remain a bit squidgy in the middle.

About 10 minutes before the pudding is done, put the cream, butter, sugar and salt in a saucepan over a low heat. Bring to the boil, reduce the heat and simmer for 5–7 minutes, until thickened and dark.

As soon as it comes out of the oven, use a fork or skewer to pierce the pudding a few times. Pour over half the sauce and give it a few minutes to sink in. To serve, cut into slices, pour over more sauce and serve immediately with vanilla ice cream.

# Molten chocolate, coffee and cardamom pots

This rich and indulgent dessert takes inspiration from the endless cups of aromatic, cardamom-infused black coffee that Palestinians drink all day. It is a majestic food pairing, with the warm and spicy notes of the ground cardamom complementing the bitter coffee perfectly. So, I thought, why not add chocolate? You can make the batter ahead of time and simply pop the pots into the oven shortly ahead of serving. You will need 6 ramekins.

**Serves 6**

3 tablespoons/50g unsalted butter, plus more for the ramekins
7 oz./200g good-quality dark chocolate
1/2 cup plus 2 tablespoons/ 120g superfine sugar

3 eggs
pinch of fine sea salt
1 teaspoon cocoa powder
1/4 cup/50g all-purpose flour
3 cardamom pods
1/2 teaspoon instant coffee

Preheat the oven to 400°F/200°C and lightly butter 6 ramekins.

Break the chocolate into small pieces and place in a heatproof bowl. Sit this bowl over a pan of simmering water (don't let the base touch the water) and allow the chocolate to melt, stirring occasionally. Set aside and leave to cool.

Cream the butter and sugar together with an electric mixer, then beat in the eggs, one at a time, the salt, cocoa powder and flour. Remove the seeds from the cardamom pods, grind them to a powder in a mortar and pestle and add them to the batter. Then mix the coffee granules with 1 tablespoon just-boiled water until dissolved and stir that in, too. Finally, add the melted chocolate and blend until smooth.

Gently spoon the batter into the prepared ramekins. You can cover and put them to one side (or store in the fridge) if you aren't cooking them right away. Otherwise, bake in the oven for 12–13 minutes, until they are just firm. Serve immediately, with vanilla ice cream.

# Semolina and rose water slice

NAMOURA

This is a sweet and sticky teatime treat, fragranced with aromatic rose water and a warming cardamom syrup. *Namoura* is rich and dense, one of those cakes that always has you reaching for one more small piece. Enjoy it with little cups of tea infused with sage, or with cardamom coffee, for a truly authentic experience. It keeps well for 3–4 days in an airtight container. I use a 12 x 8 in./30 x 20cm baking pan for this.

**Makes about 24 slices, depending on size**

FOR THE NAMOURA
2 tablespoons tahini
6 cardamom pods
2 cups/350g semolina
1 cup/235g unflavored yogurt
¼ cup/50g superfine sugar
1½ teaspoons baking powder
¼ teaspoon fine sea salt
1 teaspoon rose water
2 tablespoons flaked almonds

FOR THE SYRUP
1¼ cups/300g sugar
1 teaspoon lemon juice
1 tablespoon rose water

Coat the inside of a 12 x 8 in./30 x 20cm baking pan with the tahini.

Remove the seeds from the cardamom pods and grind them to a powder in a mortar and pestle. Place in a large bowl and add the semolina, yogurt, sugar, baking powder, salt and rose water. Mix well, then spoon the mixture into the prepared baking pan and, using the back of a wet metal spoon, smooth the surface of the pudding.

Slice the cake into squares or diamonds and dot each piece with a few flaked almonds. Cover with plastic wrap and leave to rest at room temperature for 1 hour.

Preheat the oven to 350°F/180°C. Bake for 30–40 minutes, or until golden brown.

Meanwhile, make the syrup. Dissolve the sugar in 1 cup/250ml water and the lemon juice in a saucepan placed over a medium heat, then bring it to a gentle simmer for 5 minutes. Take off the heat and stir in the rose water. Leave to cool.

As soon as the cake comes out of the oven, pour over the syrup and cut the *namoura* into squares or diamonds once more. Leave to cool completely before removing from the pan.

# Banana and tahini ice cream with date syrup

This silky and creamy dessert is the easiest ice cream you will ever make and, without a doubt, the most healthful. Freezing the bananas and then blending them gives you a wonderfully rich, soft-scoop ice cream texture without the need for dairy, added sugar or an ice-cream maker. Tahini gives it a Palestinian twist and the date syrup and sesame seeds add an addictive depth of flavor. Start this the day before you want to serve it, for the best results.

**Serves 4**

4 large, ripe bananas
2 tablespoons tahini
½ teaspoon fine sea salt

2 tablespoons date syrup
2 teaspoons white or black
sesame seeds

Peel the bananas, cut them into chunks, then place them in a freezable airtight container. Freeze the bananas for at least 2 hours, or preferably overnight.

In a food processor, blend the frozen banana pieces with the tahini and salt. You'll probably need to scrape down the sides a few times to get it evenly blended. Keep processing until you get a smooth soft-serve ice cream-like texture. Return to the airtight container and freeze for at least another 2 hours.

To serve, scoop into glasses, drizzle with some date syrup and add a scattering of sesame seeds.

# Knafeh

The glorious love child of baklava and cheesecake, *knafeh* is exactly as delicious and rib-sticking as that sounds. It is believed to have originated in Nablus, a vibrant Palestinian city in the heart of the West Bank and, on my visits there, I've seen vendors serving up freshly baked portions of the warm, gooey dessert on practically every street corner. It is made with shredded filo pastry (*kadaif*) that you can easily pick up in Middle Eastern or Turkish stores. Use a baking dish around 9½ in./24cm square for the best results.

**Serves 6**

**FOR THE SYRUP**
1 cup/200g superfine sugar
1 tablespoon lemon juice
1 tablespoon rose water or orange blossom water

**FOR THE KNAFEH**
14 oz./400g *kadaif* pastry
1¾ sticks/200g salted butter, melted
14 oz./400g *akkawi* cheese, grated, or 7 oz./200g grated mozzarella mixed with 7 oz./200g ricotta crushed unsalted pistachios, to serve

Preheat the oven to 400°F/200°C.

Start with the syrup. Pour 1 cup/250ml water into a saucepan and add the sugar and lemon juice. Place over a medium heat and bring to a gentle simmer. Let it bubble away, stirring occasionally, for 5 minutes. Take it off the heat, stir in the flower water and leave to cool. The syrup must be completely cold when it is poured over the *kadaif* pastry, or it will become soggy.

Blitz the *kadaif* in a food processor until it resembles coarse crumbs. Butter the sides of a 9½ in./24cm square baking dish, then rub the rest of the butter into the blitzed pastry with your hands.

Spread one-third of the pastry into the prepared dish, top with the cheese, then spread the remaining pastry on top, making sure the cheese is evenly covered.

Bake for around 35 minutes, or until golden brown.

As soon as the *knafeh* comes out of the oven, pour the syrup evenly over it. Sprinkle it with crushed pistachios, then cut into pieces and serve warm.

# Chocolate and tahini cookies

These are inspired by the chocolate and sesame *halawa* that I always enjoy thickly spread on toasted bread on my trips to the OPT. Like most cookie recipes, this is straightforward to make, but what makes all the difference to the texture is leaving the dough to rest for a few hours (or even overnight) so, if you can, plan ahead.

**Makes 12**

1 stick/120g unsalted butter
½ cup/90g light brown sugar
½ cup/90g superfine sugar
1 egg, plus 1 egg yolk
4 tablespoons tahini
1 teaspoon vanilla extract
1¼ cups/180g all-purpose flour
½ teaspoon baking soda

½ teaspoon baking powder
¼ teaspoon fine sea salt
¼ teaspoon ground cinnamon
3 tablespoons/25g cocoa powder
6 oz./170g good-quality dark chocolate, roughly chopped

Melt the butter in a small saucepan, then let it cool down for 5 minutes. Put both sugars into a bowl, gently pour over the melted butter and beat well with an electric mixer.

Add the egg and egg yolk, tahini and vanilla and beat until light and creamy.

Slowly stir in the flour, baking soda, baking powder, salt and cinnamon and beat together. Finally, sift in the cocoa powder, then fold in the dark chocolate pieces. Stir to combine, but don't worry if there are as few streaks of cocoa, as these will cause a nice rippled effect. Cover and leave the dough to rest for at least 1 hour, or overnight.

When you are ready to bake the cookies, preheat the oven to 350°F/180°C and line 2 large baking sheets with parchment paper.

Use a dessert spoon or an ice cream scoop to spoon 12 balls of the cookie dough onto the prepared baking sheets, leaving an inch around each ball. Pop into the oven and bake for about 15 minutes.

Cool the cookies on the baking sheets for 5 minutes before carefully transferring to wire racks with a spatula.

# Little date cookies

MA'AMOUL

These rich semolina shortbread cookies filled with date paste, warming spices and aromatic rose water are an essential part of the Palestinian Ramadan and Easter celebrations. For best results, use a *ma'amoul* mold, which makes it simple to craft the cookies into decorative shapes. They are available online and make beautiful, dainty cookies. These will keep for up to 4 days in an airtight container.

**Makes 25**

### FOR THE DOUGH
3 cups/500g semolina
1/3 cup/75g all-purpose flour
2 sticks/250g unsalted butter, melted and cooled
1/2 cup/85g superfine sugar
1/4 teaspoon fine sea salt
4 tablespoons whole milk
2 tablespoons rose water

### FOR THE FILLING
9 oz./300g Medjool dates, pitted and roughly chopped
1/2 teaspoon ground cinnamon
1/4 teaspoon freshly grated nutmeg
1/4 teaspoon ground allspice seeds from 4 cardamom pods, crushed
1 tablespoon rose water
1/4 teaspoon fine sea salt
confectioner's sugar, to dust (optional)

Begin by mixing the semolina, flour, butter, sugar and salt in a food processor or electric mixer until you get texture akin to crumbs. (You can also use your hands to rub in the butter.) Then add the milk and rose water and mix until a soft dough forms. Wrap in plastic wrap and leave to rest for 1 hour in the fridge.

Make the filling: place all the ingredients, except the confectioner's sugar, in a food processor and blitz until smooth. Cover and chill for 30 minutes.

Preheat the oven to 400°F/200°C and line a large baking sheet with parchment paper.

Divide the dough into 25 balls. Pick up a ball and press your finger into the dough, creating a small hole. Place 1/2 teaspoon of date mixture into the hole, pinch the sides to encase the filling, then roll it back into a ball. If you have a *ma'amoul* mold, lightly press the ball into it, push it down and then tap or gently pry it out onto the baking sheet. Otherwise, just flatten the ball slightly into a thick disc and use the back of a fork to press a pattern into the top. Repeat to fill and shape the remaining cookies.

Bake for 20 minutes, or until golden on top. Cool on a wire rack before serving, dusted with a little confectioner's sugar, if you like.

# Coconut bites

Chewy and moist on the inside, crispy and golden on the outside, these delicious coconut cookies are found in bakeries throughout Palestine. I enjoy them plain, but they are even more irresistible when dipped in chocolate. These keep for about 3 days in an airtight container.

**Makes 12**

2½ cups/200g shredded coconut
¾ cup/175g superfine sugar
4 egg whites
¼ teaspoon fine sea salt

1 teaspoon vanilla extract
2 oz./60g good-quality dark chocolate, roughly chopped (optional)

Preheat the oven to 350°F/180°C. Line a large baking sheet with parchment paper.

Place all the ingredients, except the chocolate, in a medium-sized saucepan and set over a low heat. Stir the mixture continuously with a wooden spoon for 6-8 minutes until all the sugar has dissolved and the batter starts to stick together in a thick paste. Take off the heat and leave the mixture to cool for 5 minutes.

Use a spoon to scoop 12 evenly sized balls onto the prepared sheet.

Bake for 10-15 minutes, until the cookies have just started to turn golden.

If you want to add the chocolate, wait until the coconut bites have cooled completely, then melt the chocolate by placing it in a medium heatproof bowl set over a saucepan of simmering water (don't let the base touch the water), stirring occasionally until melted and smooth.

Dip the bottom (the flat side) of each cookie into the melted chocolate, then place them, dipped side down, back on the lined baking sheet. Refrigerate until the chocolate hardens.

# Oranges with orange blossom water and pistachios

Simplicity is the best way to end a meal and this fragrant orange dessert, perfumed with delicate flower water, is perfect when you want a lighter note with which to finish a feast. Use blood oranges when in season for a more visually striking plate and feel free to substitute the orange blossom water with rose water, as it works just as well.

**Serves 4**

5 unwaxed or organic oranges
2 tablespoons mild honey, or to taste
1 tablespoon orange blossom water

2 tablespoons roughly crushed unsalted pistachios
mint leaves, to serve (optional)
Greek yogurt, mascarpone, or crème fraîche, to serve (optional)

Zest one of the oranges, then cut it in half and squeeze its juice. Place the zest and juice in a bowl and stir in the honey and orange blossom water.

Using a small knife, cut the peel and white pith from the remaining oranges. Do this by slicing the top and bottom off the first one, cutting deep enough that you see a wheel of orange flesh on both sides. Place the orange on one of its flat ends, then slice off the remaining peel and pith, following the contour of the fruit. Now slice across into ½ in./1cm-thick rounds. Repeat with the remaining oranges. Arrange the slices on a plate and spoon over the orange blossom syrup.

Taste for sweetness and add more honey, if you want. Top with the pistachios and add a smattering of mint leaves, if using. Serve with yogurt, mascarpone or crème fraîche, if you like.

# Baklava

These classic sticky, nutty Middle Eastern squares are very easy to make and the basic recipe is one you can play with, adapting the nuts and spices to your preference. This recipe is inspired by my visit to the Alsadaqa patisserie in Nazareth, an enchanting family-run business that sells a stunning selection of Palestinian sweets (see page 245). I was invited into their kitchen to help hand-roll a yard-long log of bright green pistachio filo sweets; quite the entertaining scene, as let's just say I lacked the "magic touch" of the Sahleh family who run the bakery. This recipe, however, is easy enough for even a baklava novice like me to get right and is wonderful served as an afternoon treat alongside black tea or coffee.

Use a square pan about 9 in./23cm in size and a pastry brush for coating each filo sheet in butter. As you will be cutting through the baklava, I'd avoid using a non-stick cake pan, as you may score and damage it.

**Serves 8**

FOR THE SYRUP
¾ cup/175g sugar
1 tablespoon lemon juice

FOR THE BAKLAVA
2 ⅓ cups/250g walnuts
¼ teaspoon ground cinnamon

pinch of fine sea salt
5 tablespoons/75g salted butter, melted, plus more for the pan
15 sheets of filo pastry
pistachio nibs, to serve

Place the syrup ingredients in a saucepan with 1 cup/250ml water and bring to a gentle simmer. Let it bubble away, stirring occasionally, for 5 minutes, then leave to cool. It must be completely cold when poured over the filo, or the pastry will become soggy.

Preheat the oven to 400°F/200°C.

Grind the walnuts in a food processor until they are extremely fine. Mix with the cinnamon and salt.

Lightly butter a 9 in./23cm square baking pan, ideally non-stick. Layer 5 sheets of filo into the pan, brushing each with melted butter as you go. Then spoon over half the walnut mixture. Repeat with another 5 layers of filo, buttering each sheet as you go, then add the remaining walnuts. Finish with the final 5 layers of filo, again buttering each sheet, and taking care to generously butter the top layer. Cut the baklava into diamonds with a sharp knife, ensuring the blade goes right to the bottom of the pan.

Bake for 30–40 minutes, or until golden brown and crisp.

Remove the baklava from the oven and immediately spoon half the cold syrup over the top. Leave for a few minutes for the syrup to soak in, then pour over the remaining syrup. Scatter with the pistachios.

Allow the baklava to cool completely before removing individual pieces from the dish with a spatula.

These will keep for 3–4 days in an airtight container. Don't store them in the fridge, or they will harden.

# Nazareth and The Galilee

In the dark, cool wine cellar under his family home, Nemi Ashkar poured me a large glass of ruby red Cabernet Sauvignon. I sniffed, inhaling hints of blackcurrant, plum and vanilla and, when I tilted my glass to my mouth to take a sip, the richness of oak and spiciness of black pepper warmed the back of my throat. "Wow!" I exclaimed, more than a little surprised. "This is really good!" Nemi smiled. "Of course it is, it's wine from The Galilee."

The Galilee has been producing wine for several millennia and, most famously, it was here that Jesus is believed to have performed his very first miracle: turning water into wine. Today, Nemi is using wine to reconnect with his family's history and heritage, having established a winery that uses grapes from Iqrit, the village where his family are from.

Nemi grew up hearing stories about his ancestors' exile from Iqrit where, in November 1948, the Israeli army evacuated the whole town. Many villagers took just basic necessities with them, thinking they would only be gone for two weeks, but the area was subsequently declared a military zone and the villagers were forbidden to return. The people of Iqrit took their case to Israel's supreme court, which ruled in July 1951 that their evacuation was illegal and they must be permitted to return, but on Christmas Eve of that year Israeli soldiers demolished the village, leaving only the church and the cemetery intact. "We have

been trying to get back to our land ever since," Nemi told me. "We are refugees in our own country."

Wine had always been cultivated in Iqrit so, when Nemi developed a passion for wine production after spending time working in California, he decided to use his skills to try and revitalize the Palestinian wine industry. "Wine to us is passion," he says. "It's family and friends. It's warmth of heart and generosity of spirit. Good wine is the essence of civilization."

After pursuing a career in tech with several postings in Silicon Valley, Nemi completed a number of wine production courses in California's Napa Valley. Back in The Galilee, he started investigating how he could grow grapes on his ancestral land. "Because I'm a Palestinian citizen of Israel, I'm not allowed to lease or buy the land, so I worked with an Israeli man and he put his name on the paperwork."

Ashkar Winery, as his family business is now called, has become a great success, receiving rave reviews, and demand now far outstrips production. For Nemi and his family though, success isn't just about the high quality of the wine, it is about paying testament to the ancient connection between their forefathers and their land, with the hope that one day they will be able to return to it. "The irony is that it is only when we die that Israel will permit us to go back to Iqrit," says Nemi. "They allow us to bury the dead in the local cemetery."

After polishing off another glass of red on Nemi's balcony, I headed upstairs to cook with his wife Amira. She showed me how to make sweet cheese and walnut pastries and a signature Galilean dish, *bamiyeh*, okra braised with tomatoes and laden with thick slices of young garlic. We ate it with herb-packed tabbouleh that we scooped up with crunchy Romaine lettuce and raw cabbage leaves, and washed it all down with small glasses of milky-white arak made from local grapes and anise, before cracking open another bottle of wine to enjoy on that warm summer evening.

—

Nazareth is the largest city in The Galilee, bustling with shop-lined streets, blaring car horns, traffic jams and young men with a penchant for showing off at the wheel. It's a predominantly Palestinian city, known both as the "Arab capital of Israel" and for culinary innovation, hosting a new generation of chefs who are revolutionizing the local food scene.

One of those is Johnny Goric, head chef at the Legacy Hotel. Trained in France, Johnny now brings Western techniques to the cuisine of his home country, creating modern interpretations of Palestinian classic recipes. He invited me into his kitchen to watch him making *shish barak*, little lamb dumplings, cooked in a rich yogurt sauce.

Like many chefs around the world, Johnny is decorated with tattoos and, being of Palestinian-Armenian descent, he has one that he was particularly keen to show me. Rolling up his sleeve, he revealed an inked prayer in Aramaic that runs up his forearm. 'This is the language of Jesus,' he said proudly. 'My family's lineage goes back to his time.'

But Johnny is certainly not stuck in the past and, at the Legacy, he is creating dishes that celebrate modern flavors. At the entrance to the restaurant he stopped to show me a mural on the wall, depicting four scenes from Jesus's life, and it's clear that he takes inspiration in his cooking from these biblical stories. "There is nothing more important than breaking bread with others," he told me. "We are taught this from Jesus's last supper. Sharing food and wine with people is important, even if you are in conflict with someone or think you are being betrayed."

In the kitchen, Johnny immersed himself in the tasks at hand, forehead furrowed in concentration as he stuffed the little dumplings with small spoonfuls of ground lamb. "Being a great chef is about knowing where you come from," he told me, sliding the dumplings into the yogurt broth. "It starts with your mother's cooking, then you add layers."

Working with lesser-used local ingredients is part of Johnny's signature style and he tries to incorporate ingredients such as mustard seeds, capers and basil that grow wild in the hills of The Galilee and are not traditionally used in Palestinian cooking.

"I know that the Occupation has damaged our food culture in many ways, but I'm not just sitting and wiping away tears," he told me as he assembled toasted garlic chips, mint oil and micro-herbs for plating the dumplings. "If anything, it motivates me to look closer to home and think about how we can best use the ingredients from our land in new and exciting ways. I want the world to recognize Palestinian food as one of the great cuisines of the globe and see what we can produce, with the basic goods that we have and using the wonderful produce that grows around us."

—

Preparing meals with locally grown produce is a common feature in all Palestinian cooking but, perhaps because of the sheer abundance of fertile soil in The Galilee, the diversity of ingredients and emphasis on plant-based food seems at its greatest here. On our way to visit a sumac farm, we drove on winding roads that circle up through the green mountains, spotting figs so ripe they were almost bursting off their branches, juicy peaches turning yellow as they ripened in the sun, and small, dark baby pomegranates just beginning to make their journey into the world.

Sumac is one of the region's most prized ingredients and is used to add a sharp and astringent kick to dishes. We arrived at the farm to be greeted by the owner, Eliyah Haddad, a sprightly 70-year-old with a raspy voice and a rugged demeanor, who traversed with such great speed and vigor up and down the hills of the farm that we struggled to keep up with him. He took us past cacti sprouting prickly pears, plum trees weighed down with purple fruit and rose bushes blooming with pink and crimson flowers, before finally arriving at the sumac orchard. There we picked at the clusters of beige berries with thumbs and forefingers, massaging them gently until they released their sticky juices. The season's harvest had already begun in earnest and the ground was covered with plastic sheets filled with sumac berries that had been left to dry under the sun. Once all their liquid has evaporated, they are transferred to a mill in one of the sheds, where they are ground into a fine powder ready to be added to stews, pastries, grilled meat dishes or salads.

—

Foraged ingredients that grow wild around The Galilee have formed the bedrock of many of the region's recipes and, the next day, I was invited to cook with Sally Azzam, one of the co-ordinators of the LIWAN, an arts and cultural center in the Old City in Nazareth. She taught me how to cook purslane (*farfahina* in Arabic), one of the most beloved foraged dishes of Palestinian cuisine. "*Farfahina* is a peasant dish," Sally told me, as we sat around a table, stripping the round green leaves from their branches. "For me, it's the foodstuff that reminds me most of our land. Many refugees who had to

flee from their homes in 1948 survived on this weed, because it grew wild everywhere and still does. It kept them alive as they were on their journey of exile so, for me, it has a special and poignant significance."

Sally is strong and articulate, and her blue eyes shone with determination, her voice occasionally breaking with emotion as she talked me through the history of food production and cultivation in The Galilee and how it has changed. "You know," she said, leaning in as if to share a secret. "Knowing how to cook is power. I remember being under curfew in the first *intifada* (the Palestinian uprising of the late 1980s) and after a few days, we ran out of food in our house. When you run out of bread, what do you do? You need to know how to make it. Cooking is essential for our survival."

We moved on to chopping onions and slicing garlic, gently frying both in olive oil while we diced tomatoes. "But plants can also be used to damage land," Sally sighed sadly, stirring the onions at the bottom of the pan so they didn't catch. "After 1948, many pine trees were planted by Israeli officials to cover the remains of Palestinian houses. The tragedy was that not only did they cover our history, but they destroyed the soil, as pine trees make it too acidic to grow food."

Sally asked me to keep an eye on the *farfahina* as she set the table, bringing over large discs of still-warm *taboon* bread from a local bakery and a remarkable sweet and salty tapenade spread made from black olives

and honey. As we sat down to eat with her husband and the center's staff, I told her the *farfahina* dish felt very rooted in this place and not something I could recreate at home, where foraging purslane isn't so common. "That's okay," she laughed. "Maybe you should tell people to come here and see it for themselves; we want people to visit us here, so they can get a real taste of Palestine."

—

Soft, sticky, syrup-drenched pastries are among my favorite types of desserts, so when I heard that Nazareth is famed for its sweet pastry shops, I knew I was in for a treat. Along with my photographer Raya, I headed in the direction of Alsadaqa bakery, which purportedly makes the city's best baklava, and was greeted at the door by Suliman Sahleh, who has been working in the bakery since he was 15. Suliman swiftly whisked us round the shop and, in five minutes of flurry, I was introduced to at least a dozen relatives—uncles, aunts and cousins—who make up the friendly team of this family business, which has served up sweet baked goods to the people of Nazareth since 1973.

*Alsadaqa* means "friendship" in Arabic and the shop makes 42 different kinds of baklava. With Suliman's encouragement, I tried as many of those as I could. From the classic walnut and cinnamon diamonds, to pastries filled with dried apricots and figs, to a coconut and pistachio filo roll thickened with layers of luscious coconut cream, the creativity and

inventiveness made each pastry truly joyful to eat. The atmosphere of the café adjoining the bakery matched the quality of the sweets—it was lively and convivial, full of families enjoying themselves—and I was not in the least bit surprised to hear that they sell 1,500kg of baklava every week and are one of the most popular establishments in town.

After feasting on probably a few more pieces of baklava than was strictly necessary, I followed Suliman to the bakery's kitchens... where I walked into a cloud of flour. All around me, thin sheets of filo were being stretched and pulled, and I wandered over to a corner of the room where a bright green log of pistachio baklava was being rolled. With Suliman's guidance, I attempted to fold and roll the delicate pastry over itself, concentrating on trying to keep the ground nuts contained and the roll in an even shape. After a few valiant efforts, we all agreed it was probably best if I left the baklava-making to the professionals, so we walked back to the main shop, where members of the Sahleh family dragged us behind the counter, posing for selfies and insisting that we sample even more sweets.

As we moved around the shop in a sugar-laden, laughing frenzy, Raya paused from taking photographs and looked up at me. "You know, this is the kind of place where you can taste the deliciousness of the baklava before it even comes near your mouth," she said. "Just look at the fun they have when they are making it!"

# Menu planning

Palestinian meals have a flexible approach to courses, with smaller and larger dishes often placed on the table at the same time and diners helping themselves to as much as they want. Cooked and fresh vegetables are a central component and complement heartier meat and rice dishes, so try to serve several vegetable sides for texture and brightness. There will always be certain staples with every meal, so you would do well to have these on hand: a fresh salad, thick unflavored yogurt and, of course, olives. I like to start meals with with small bowls of olive oil and za'atar, for dipping bread.

# Index of dairy-free, gluten-free and vegan recipes

## SALADS

Roast Romanesco cauliflower with tahini and pomegranates 78
Everyday Palestinian salad 81
Roast rainbow carrots with herbed yogurt 84
Gazan salad 85
Donyana salad 91
Eggplant, tomato and pomegranate salad 92
Radicchio, radish and clementine salad 95
Red pepper, lentil and tomato salad 98

## SOUPS

Roast cauliflower soup 115
Arugula soup 119
Lentil soup with walnut and cilantro smash 120

## MAIN COURSES

Roast eggplant with spiced chickpeas and tomatoes 136
Upside-down rice with eggplants and peppers 142
Lentil, eggplant and pomegranate stew 144
Comforting spinach and chickpeas 147
Stuffed cabbage rolls 148
Gazan lentils with Swiss chard and tahini 151
Lemon, cumin and green chilli sea bass 154
Za'atar roast salmon with garlicky bean mash 157
Spicy shrimp and tomato stew 158
Roast chicken stuffed with raisins and pine nuts 174
Spiced chicken with dried lime pilaf 176
Chicken shawarma 177
Gazan beef, chickpeas and Swiss chard 182
Slow-roast shoulder of lamb with Palestinian spices 189
Stuffed zucchini with spiced beef or lamb 190
Lamb meatballs with tahini 192

## DESSERTS

Apricot and rose water rice pudding 215
Banana and tahini ice cream with date syrup 226
Coconut bites 232
Oranges with orange blossom water and pistachios 235

# VEGAN

## MAZZEH

Hummus 22
Hummus with lemon and green chilli chickpeas 26
Charred eggplant with tahini 28
"Almost za'atar" 36
Dukkah 36
Arabic flatbreads 41
Herbed focaccia 43
Roast red peppers with olives and capers 44
Roast okra with spicy tomatoes 47
Lemon and chilli roast potatoes 49
Green beans with olive oil 50
Falafel 61
Quick pickled avocados 63
Pickled turnips with beet 64
Pickled cucumbers 66
Pickled cauliflower and carrots 67

## SALADS

Roast Romanesco cauliflower with tahini and pomegranates 78
Everyday Palestinian salad 81
Gazan salad 85
Tabbouleh 88
Donyana salad 91
Eggplant, tomato and pomegranate salad 92
Radicchio, radish and clementine salad 95
Chickpea and bulgur salad 101

## SOUPS

Red lentil and squash soup with za'atar croutons 117
Lentil soup with walnut and cilantro smash 120
Kale, fennel and noodle soup 123

## MAIN COURSES

Roast eggplant with spiced chickpeas and tomatoes 136
Lentil, eggplant and pomegranate stew 144
Comforting spinach and chickpeas 147
Stuffed cabbage rolls 148
Gazan lentils with Swiss chard and tahini 151
Brown rice and lentil pilaf with crispy fried onions 152

## DESSERTS

Banana and tahini ice cream with date syrup 226

# Index

# Acknowledgments

Thanks for Raya Manaa' for her wit, passion, hospitality and warmth. Her love of food and dedication to celebrating Palestinian culture made her the perfect partner on this journey.

Thanks also to Hosam Salem for sharing his beautiful photography, which gave me a glimpse of the Gaza I could not visit.

To all the Palestinians I cooked with, ate with, interviewed and talked to, thank you for inspiring me with your resilience and humour and teaching me about hope, community and justice.

Thanks to my agent Clare Hulton and to the wonderful team at Bloomsbury: Natalie Bellos, Xa Shaw Stewart, Lisa Pendreigh, Ellen Williams, Thi Dinh, Jen Hampson and Lena Hall. I appreciate your support and encouragement immensely. Special thanks to Lucy Bannell, whose insights, moral support and magical way with words helped me craft the best possible version of this book. Thanks to Caroline Clark for her beautiful design and to Matt Russell, Rosie Reynolds and Jennifer Kay for making the food look so damn delicious. Thanks to Lucinda Ganderton for the wonderful embroidery on the cover of the book, and Andrew Lyons who has done a great job with the map of Palestine. And a special shout-out to Catherine Phipps for helping me to perfect some of the recipes with her scrupulous testing and sage advice.

And last but not least, thanks to Kasia Kmeick, Mike Podmore, Louise De Villiers, Natasha Moskovici, Maryam Khan, Chris Jennings, Fati Rabiee and Asaf Khan for accompanying me on the journey of writing this book and for always having unbridled enthusiasm for recipe testing and second helpings. Dinner at yours next, okay?

YASMIN KHAN is an author, food and travel writer and cook who is passionate about sharing people's stories through food. Her debut book, *The Saffron Tales*, celebrated her culinary adventures through Iran and was named by the *New York Times*, the *Wall Street Journal* and the BBC's *Food Programme* as one of the best cookbooks of 2016. Before working in food, Yasmin trained in law and was a human rights campaigner for a decade, running national and international campaigns for NGOs and grassroots groups. yasminkhanstories.com
instagram.com/yasminkhanstories
twitter.com/yasmin_khan

MATT RUSSELL is a photographer and director based in London. mattrussell.co.uk

RAYA MANAA' is a photographer based in Haifa. rayamanaa.com
instagram.com/rayamanaa

HOSAM SALEM is a photojournalist based in Gaza. instagram.com/hosalem

First American Edition 2019

Originally published in Great Britain under the title *Zaitoun: Recipes and Stories from the Palestinian Kitchen*

For information about permission to reproduce selections from this book, write to Permissions, W. W. Norton & Company, Inc., 500 Fifth Avenue, New York, NY 10110

For information about special discounts for bulk purchases, please contact W. W. Norton Special Sales at specialsales@wwnorton.com or 800-233-4830

ISBN 978-1-324-00262-8

W. W. Norton & Company, Inc.
500 Fifth Avenue, New York, N.Y. 10110
www.wwnorton.com

W. W. Norton & Company Ltd.
15 Carlisle Street, London W1D 3BS

1 2 3 4 5 6 7 8 9 0